# Nantucket Cuisine Cookbook

*Happy Cooking!*

*Ellen Brown*

# Nantucket Cuisine Cookbook

by Ellen Brown

Illustrated by Rose Gonnella

FARAWAY
PUBLISHING
GROUP

FARAWAY PUBLISHING GROUP

Copyright © 2002 by Ellen Brown. All rights reserved. Printed in the United States of America.
No part of this book may be reproduced or transmitted in any form or by any means, electronic
or mechanical, including photocopying, recording, or by an information storage and retrieval
system, without written permission from the publisher.

Illustrations by Rose Gonnella.
All images of Nantucket scenery accompanying still-life drawings, the illustration accompanying
the table of contents, and chapter ten, first appeared in "*summer nantucket drawings*,"
© 1995 Rose Gonnella/Waterborn Group.

ISBN 0-9720457-0-8

Published by Faraway Publishing Group, P.O. Box 792, Nantucket, MA 02554

Library of Congress Cataloging-in-Publication Data is available.

10  9  8  7  6  5  4  3  2  1

First Edition

Cover and interior designed by [work]
Printed by Studley Press, Massachusetts

# Dedication

This book is dedicated to the memory of my father, who introduced me to the magic of small towns by the sea.

# Acknowledgments

While writing a book is a solitary task, its publication is always a team effort. My deepest thanks go:

To Nancy Martin, publisher and dear friend, for suggesting I spend the quiet winter months writing this book, and for her steadfast insistence on maintaining the high quality of every aspect of its creation;

To Rose Gonnella, artist extraordinaire, whose sensitive and lyrical drawings so enliven these pages;

To Susan Derecskey, superb copy editor, for her encouragement as well as meticulous attention to detail;

To Alejandro Medina and Cesar Rubin, the team from [work], for their inspired design and interior layout;

To Ann Brody Cove and Don Weadon, long-time friends and Nantucket Cuisine board members, for their support and encouragement to start the business three years ago;

And to the late Samantha Cat Brown, my beloved companion for fifteen years, for her unconditional love during the hundreds of hours spent with me at the computer or in the kitchen eating the mistakes.

# Introduction

*"Nantucket! Take out your map and look at it. See what a real corner of the world it occupies; how it stands there away off shore."*

Herman Melville, *Moby-Dick*

The island's geographic isolation "away off shore" defines both its environment and its food.

I've titled this the *Nantucket Cuisine Cookbook* because Nantucket Cuisine is the name of the catering business I launched in 2000. However, the name also describes my cooking style as it has evolved during the past decade since I began living here.

Do not be intimidated by the word "cuisine." Think of these easy dishes as "Nantucket Cooking." Since I've written recipes for home cooks for almost thirty years, the recipes in this book are not fussy food that requires advanced cooking skills or specialized equipment. These are real dishes that can be cooked by real people.

The majority of these recipes contain fewer than a dozen ingredients. Simplicity, reflected physically on the island by cedar shake houses and cobblestone streets, is one of the basic tenets of life on Nantucket. It also underscores the dishes in this book.

The creation of Nantucket Cuisine is the merger of a unique set of factors that comprise this special place. It is a blend of the island's indigenous foods, spirit, and history.

American cooking in all regions is defined by the juxtaposition of the culinary heritage of the settlers who joined the continent's Native American population, and the foods they found or could grow. Coastal New England cooking shares such foods as lobster, clams, cranberries, and blueberries. In addition to these foods, Nantucket cooking is distinguished by dishes that utilize prized bay scallops, as well as some Portuguese influences introduced by sailors during the whaling era.

At the center of the island's spirit is a reverence for nature, and that principle forms the foundation of my cooking. I choose the best seasonal ingredients from the land and the sea, and glorify their inherent flavors. Since the fish and seafood recipes were developed with species caught in local waters, substitutions are offered for cooks living in other regions.

My respect for nature extends to cooking seasonally, even though modern transportation has provided us with a new definition of "airline food." While it is possible to find fresh blueberries in January, I would rather reserve my enjoyment of them for July when they can be picked locally. The first fresh corn and tomatoes ripened on the vine in August are as much a marker of the progression of the year as the first sight of daffodils, the harbingers of spring.

Professional cooks have year-round access to a veritable cornucopia of foods supplied by specialty food vendors. However, all of the recipes in the *Nantucket Cuisine Cookbook* were tested from the contents of Nantucket's markets in winter, when the options are extremely lean. Locating the ingredients for these recipes will be no problem, regardless of where you live.

Along with its spirit, the island's history as the world's whaling capital in the early nineteenth century is another factor underpinning Nantucket Cuisine. The whaling boats circumnavigated the globe, and the sailors' palates were elevated to appreciate foods beyond bland, traditional New England cookery drawn from Anglo-Saxon roots. They returned from their voyages with spices and culinary memories from the South Pacific, Asia, South America, and the Caribbean.

My dishes are influenced by these same foods from sun-drenched coasts. I like bold flavors, not meek ones. Foods from these regions also meet today's desire for dishes that are light and healthful but not at the expense of flavor.

Vibrant color also characterizes foods from these equatorial regions. Eating is a totally sensual experience that utilizes senses beyond the obvious one of taste. One of my tenets of recipe development is that dishes should be visually appealing, and contain a distinctive mix of textures and colors as well as flavors.

The goal for the dishes in the *Nantucket Cuisine Cookbook* is that they can be created quickly and easily. Whenever possible I have simplified recipes through the use of readily purchased ingredients. For example, while *glace de viande*, a highly concentrated veal stock, is part of my larder, I doubt it can be found in many home kitchens. That's why Shepherd's Pie includes a package of gravy mix to give the sauce the same rich flavor provided by *glace de viande*.

When catering parties, last-minute preparation is not a consideration because the kitchen is staffed with cooks. But that is not the case when I'm cooking at home. I want all cooks to be part of their parties and not worried about last-minute cooking that takes them away from friends and family. Each recipe in the *Nantucket Cuisine Cookbook* is annotated with how far in advance a dish can be prepared, either partially or totally.

While my recipes are carefully planned, my move to the island was far more by serendipity than design. Before Nantucket, I lived in Washington, DC, where I moved in 1981 to become the founding food editor of *USA Today*.

Part of my job included attending cooking schools, and working in restaurant kitchens with some of the heralded young masters of modern American cooking. I learned from Wolfgang Puck how to make crisp, crunchy pizza dough and from Paul Prudhomme the nuances of Cajun cooking.

An exciting aspect of covering food on a national level was chronicling the emergence of New American Cuisine as a valid culinary movement. It began in the early 1980s as a quest to make traditional American dishes more sophisticated by employing the finesse of classic French technique. The second generation of chefs and food writers then broke down American cuisine into smaller components, and the definition of Nantucket Cuisine, reflected by the recipes within, is consistent with these subsets of regions as they have been delineated over the past decade.

In 1986, after five years at what was an exciting job, I left the rigors of daily journalism, shortly after the publication of my first cookbook, *Cooking with the New American Chefs*. Life as a freelance writer and food consultant meant that I could work anywhere I could connect a computer and a telephone, so an old dream of living on the ocean was revived. I thought wistfully about Nantucket. I had been here during my college years but had not returned for more than two decades.

I rented houses for three summers and was sustained for the rest of the year by memories of wandering down Main Street in the morning, with brilliant flowers and perfect produce arranged like still-life paintings on the backs of flatbed trucks. I purchased a house here in 1991, and by 1996 I was living on the island at least nine months of the year.

As my consulting business evolved, I spent less time at a stove and more time at a computer. I missed cooking and developing recipes. My life needed what sailors term "a course correction." I agree with famed French gastronome Brillat-Savarin, who wrote: "The discovery of a new dish does more for the happiness of mankind than the discovery of a new star." I wanted to add to the constellations. Thus, Nantucket Cuisine began as a business, and I became a year-round islander.

Living here full time, I began to appreciate fully and to anticipate many annual celebrations that punctuate island life. They go beyond national holidays, and each of them takes place at a time of the year that has its own set of seasonal foods. Some of these events, such as Daffodil Weekend in the spring and the beginning of family scalloping time in the fall, and their concomitant foods are featured in the last chapter of this book, "A Year of Island Occasions."

These are all celebrations that are intended to be shared with others. Food writer M.F.K. Fisher, who saw the beauty in a simple bowl of mashed potatoes, acknowledged the importance of sharing what we cook when she wrote: "There is a communion of more than our bodies when bread is broken and wine is drunk."

Freshness, flavor, and sharing are the spirit behind Nantucket Cuisine, no matter where you live. Happy cooking!

Ellen Brown
Nantucket, Massachusetts
October, 2002

# Table of Contents

## VIII. *All Dressed Up* : Spreads, Sauces, Dips, & Dressings

## IX. *Grand Finales* : Cakes, Pies, & Cookies

X. *A Year of Island Occasions*: Menus for a Dozen Memorable Meals

# Creative Canapés for Festive Occasions:
## Hors d'oeuvres

I was addicted to crab cakes while living near the Chesapeake Bay and adapted my favorite recipe to native lobster on Nantucket. While the recipe retains the classic spices from Old Bay, the cilantro adds a Southwestern touch.

*Larger versions of this hors d'oeuvre can serve four as an entree. Form the mixture into eight patties, and bake them at 400°F for 15 to 20 minutes.*

*A good lobster has a hard dark shell and a very lively disposition. Newly trapped lobsters can be quite ferocious and will swing their claws at you like a prizefighter. After a few days in captivity, they slow down considerably. If a lobster cannot hold its own arms in the air, it is not a good buy; it will die shortly.*

# Southwestern Miniature Lobster Cakes

[ Makes 24 ]

Vegetable oil spray

1 egg

2 tablespoons mayonnaise

3 tablespoons cracker meal

1 to 2 teaspoons Old Bay seasoning, to taste

1 pound lobster meat, finely diced

2 red bell peppers, seeds and ribs removed, very finely chopped

2 green bell peppers, seeds and ribs removed, very finely chopped

3 scallions, trimmed with all but 2 inches of green tops discarded, very finely chopped

3 tablespoons finely chopped cilantro

18

1. Heat the oven to 450°F. Cover a baking sheet with heavy-duty aluminum foil, and spray the foil with vegetable oil spray.
2. Combine the egg, mayonnaise, cracker meal, and Old Bay in a mixing bowl and whisk until well blended. Gently fold in the lobster, red peppers, green peppers, scallions, and cilantro.
3. Using a tablespoon, form the mixture into balls and then flatten them on the baking sheet into patties. Spray the tops of the patties with vegetable oil spray.
4. Bake for 10 to 12 minutes, or until lightly brown on top. Serve immediately.

*Note:* The lobster mixture can be made 1 day in advance and refrigerated, tightly covered with plastic wrap. Do not form or bake until just before serving.

# Nantucket Scallop Ceviche in Cherry Tomatoes

[ Makes 3 dozen ]

1 pound bay scallops

1 1/2 cups freshly squeezed lime juice

1/4 cup chopped cilantro

3 garlic cloves, peeled and minced

1 jalapeño chili, seeds and ribs removed and very finely chopped

One 4-ounce can chopped green chilies, drained

Salt to taste

2 pints round cherry tomatoes

1. Rinse the scallops and place them in a heavy plastic bag with the lime juice, cilantro, garlic, jalapeño, green chilies, and salt. Marinate the scallops, refrigerated, for at least 3 hours, or overnight. Drain the scallops and discard the marinade.

2. Cut the stem end off each tomato and scoop out the flesh with the small end of a melon baller. Invert the tomatoes onto paper towels to drain for 5 minutes. To serve, place 1 or 2 scallops in each tomato.

*Note:* The scallops should not be marinated for more than 24 hours. The tomatoes can be prepared 3 hours in advance and refrigerated.

This is one of my favorite holiday hors d'oeuvres, when succulent bay scallops are in season. Cherry tomatoes become a colorful holder for the spicy morsels.

*Ceviche is a South American method of preparing fish by marinating it in a citrus juice. The seafood remains raw; the texture and color are transformed, however, so that they taste and look cooked.*

When I wrote *All Wrapped Up* in 1998 the wrap craze was in its infancy, and most wraps were sandwich alternatives. I've continued to experiment with the form, and these easy-to-make wraps slice into gorgeous pinwheels with bright orange salmon surrounding a center of mixed greens.

*These wraps can also be served as part of a brunch, served like halved egg rolls. Rather than rolling them as described in the recipe, tuck in both sides of the tortillas first, then roll them firmly but gently. Cut them on the diagonal into two halves.*

*As an alternative to smoked salmon, the pinwheels can also be made with thinly sliced smoked turkey or smoked ham.*

# Southwest Smoked Salmon Pinwheels

[ Makes 2 dozen ]

1 cup Summer Tomato Salsa (page 169) or good quality refrigerated salsa (do not use bottled salsa)

1/4 pound cream cheese, softened

1/4 cup chopped cilantro

Four 8-inch flour tortillas

1/2 pound smoked salmon

2 cups mesclun salad mix or other baby greens

*1.* Drain the salsa in a strainer, pressing to extract as much liquid as possible. Combine the salsa, cream cheese, and cilantro in a mixing bowl and stir well. Wrap the tortillas in plastic wrap and microwave on HIGH (100%) for 20 to 30 seconds, or until soft and pliable.

*2.* Place the tortillas on a counter, and spread each with the cream cheese mixture. Arrange the salmon slices on the bottom half of each tortilla. Place 1/2 cup of the mesclun at the bottom edge of the tortilla on top of the salmon. Roll the tortillas firmly but gently starting at the filled edge. Place the rolls, seam side down, on a platter or ungreased baking sheet, and refrigerate for 1 hour.

*3.* Trim the end off each roll by cutting on the diagonal to remove the portion of the tortilla that does not meet and form a log. Slice each tortilla into 6 slices and serve chilled.

*Note:* The tortillas can be filled up to 6 hours in advance and refrigerated, tightly covered. Slice just before serving.

# Ginger Gravlax with Cilantro Mustard Sauce

[ Makes 24 ]

One 1 1/2 pound salmon fillet with skin attached

1 cup sugar

1 cup kosher salt

1/4 cup ground ginger

1/4 cup coarsely ground black pepper

Cilantro Mustard Sauce

1/2 cup Dijon mustard

1/3 cup honey

1/4 cup sesame oil

1/4 cup chopped cilantro

To serve:

1 thin baguette, thinly sliced and toasted, or melba toast crackers

Sprigs of cilantro

*1.* To prepare the gravlax, rinse the salmon fillet under cold water and rub your hand across the surface from the tail to the head end. Remove any small bones with tweezers. Combine the sugar, salt, ginger, and pepper. Place one third of the mixture in the bottom of a glass baking dish. Place the salmon on top and top the salmon with the remaining mixture. Cover the baking dish with a double layer of plastic wrap and place a smaller baking dish over the fillet. Weight the salmon down with 5 pounds of cans or a heavy pan. Weight the salmon for 3 hours at room temperature. Pour off any liquid that has accumulated and refrigerate the salmon for 2 days.

*2.* To prepare the sauce, whisk together the mustard, honey, sesame oil, and cilantro until smooth. Refrigerate the sauce, tightly covered.

*3.* To serve, rinse the coating off the salmon. Slice it very thin, starting at the tail end of the fillet. Form the slices into small circles and place each on a crouton or cracker. Spoon sauce into the center of the circle and garnish with a cilantro sprig.

*Note:* The salmon can be sliced up to 1 day in advance.

Traditional gravlax is a Scandinavian dish; it literally means "buried fish." The basic combination of salt and sugar—the curing agents—are part of this recipe; however, the classic dill has been replaced by pungent ginger. The Asian theme is reinforced with aromatic sesame oil and cilantro in the mustard sauce. This is not an impromptu dish, however. Please note that it must be started two days in advance.

*This dish can also be served as an appetizer. Arrange the slices on a bed of mixed greens tossed with some of the sauce and drizzle additional sauce on top of the slices. This gravlax also makes delicious wrap sandwiches. Follow the procedure for Southwest Smoked Salmon Pinwheels (page 20) and roll the tortillas around a core of mixed greens.*

Few foods say "Nantucket" as much as smoked bluefish. All fish stores sell it, many times locally smoked. While smoked bluefish pâté is a common use, I prefer to use it for these bite-size cakes that allow the hearty, succulent flavor of the fish to emerge.

*Variations of smoked fish cakes are imbedded in New England's culinary history. The earliest ones that sustained the Pilgrims in the 17th century were made with smoked cod. And Julia Child was not the first cooking guru with her surname. In Mrs. Lydia Maria Child's 1833* **The American Frugal Housewife** *she discusses at length the importance of smoked fish for winter protein.*

## Smoked Bluefish Cakes

[ Makes 2 1/2 dozen ]

1 1/2 pounds smoked bluefish

1 egg

1 egg yolk

1 1/2 teaspoons Old Bay seasoning

1 tablespoon freshly squeezed lemon juice

1 teaspoon Worcestershire sauce

1/4 cup vegetable oil

22

1. Chop or flake the bluefish into small flakes, and set aside. In a mixing bowl, beat the egg with the egg yolk, Old Bay, lemon juice, and Worcestershire sauce. Fold in the bluefish.

2. Form the mixture into 30 patties. Heat the oil in a skillet over medium heat. Add the patties, being careful not to crowd the pan, and fry for 3 minutes on a side, or until golden brown. Drain on paper towels and serve immediately.

*Note:* The cakes can be formed up to 1 day in advance and refrigerated, tightly covered with plastic wrap. Fry just before serving.

# Baked Shrimp Toast Rolls

[ Makes 3 dozen ]

Vegetable oil spray

12 slices white sandwich bread

3/4 pound raw shrimp, peeled and deveined

2 tablespoons chopped fresh ginger

1 tablespoon sesame oil

1 egg white

1 tablespoon dry sherry

2 tablespoons cornstarch

1 tablespoon soy sauce

2 scallions, trimmed, and sliced into 2-inch sections

1/3 cup finely chopped water chestnuts

Salt and freshly ground black pepper to taste

*1.* Preheat the oven to 425°F. Cover a baking sheet with heavy-duty aluminum foil and spray the foil with vegetable oil spray. Remove the crusts from the bread slices using a serrated bread knife. Roll each slice with a rolling pin until the bread slice is thin, but still pliable.

*2.* Combine the shrimp, ginger, sesame oil, egg white, sherry, cornstarch, and soy sauce in a food processor fitted with a steel blade. Puree until smooth, stopping a few times to scrape the sides of the workbowl. Add the scallions and finely chop them, pulsing. Scrape the mixture into a mixing bowl and stir in the water chestnuts. Season with salt and pepper.

*3.* Spread the bread slices out on a counter and place 1 heaping tablespoon of filling in a line across the long side of each slice. Roll the bread around the filling so that the edges meet and place the rolls, seam side down, on the prepared baking sheet. Spray the tops with vegetable oil spray.

*4.* Bake the rolls for 5 minutes, turn them over, and bake for 3 minutes more, or until browned. Cut each into 3 sections with a serrated knife, and serve immediately.

*Note:* The filling can be prepared 1 day in advance and refrigerated, tightly covered. Fill the bread and bake the rolls just before serving.

Delicate shrimp toasts have remained a vivid culinary memory since childhood trips to New York's Chinatown. This version is both lighter and easier to make, since the rolls are baked rather than fried. Serve them with Indonesian Barbecue Sauce (page 174).

*If you don't have a rolling pin, or you're using it to prop open a window, you can use a wine bottle to roll out the bread slices.*

One of the lasting off-shoots of the wrap craze is that quesadillas, drawn from Hispanic cuisines, have become a universal form. Flour tortillas now encase myriad ingredients, as long as cheese is one of them. I serve these Italian-inspired quesadillas often in the summer when tomatoes are glorious and basil grows in the garden.

*If your tortillas have turned into sheets of cardboard, do not despair. Place a wet paper towel in the bag, wrap the entire bag with plastic wrap, and microwave the tortillas as noted above. They will become pliable once again.*

# Pesto Quesadillas

[ Makes 18 pieces ]

Vegetable oil spray

Six 6-inch flour tortillas

1/2 cup pesto sauce, your favorite recipe or purchased

4 plum tomatoes, cored, seeded, and thinly sliced

1 1/2 cups arugula leaves, stemmed and rinsed

1 1/2 cups grated mozzarella cheese

*1.* Preheat the oven to 450°F. Cover a baking sheet with heavy-duty aluminum foil and spray the foil with vegetable oil spray. Wrap the tortillas in plastic wrap and microwave them on HIGH (100%) for 20 to 30 seconds, or until pliable.

*2.* Spread one half of each tortilla with the pesto sauce. Top the sauce with tomato slices, arugula leaves, and mozzarella cheese. Fold the blank side of the tortillas over the filled sides, and press with the palm of your hand or a spatula to keep them firmly closed. Arrange the quesadillas on the prepared baking sheet and spray the tops with vegetable oil spray.

*3.* Bake the quesadillas for 5 minutes. Turn them gently with a spatula and bake for 4 to 5 minutes more, or until brown and crisp. Allow them to sit for 2 minutes, then cut each into 3 sections and serve immediately.

*Note:* The quesadillas can be prepared 1 day in advance of baking them.

# Herbed Chèvre and Roasted Spirals

[ Makes 36 ]

3 red bell peppers, roasted and seeded,
  or 3 jarred roasted red peppers

1/2 pound mild chèvre, softened

2 tablespoons heavy cream

2 garlic cloves, peeled

8 sprigs of parsley, rinsed and stemmed

2 teaspoons herbes de provence

Salt and freshly ground black pepper to taste

---

1. Drain the peppers on paper towels and cut each in half. Set aside.

2. Combine the chèvre, cream, garlic, parsley, and herbes de provence in a food processor fitted with a steel blade. Puree until smooth, then scrape the mixture into a mixing bowl. Season with salt and pepper.

3. Spread the cheese onto the pepper halves and roll them lengthwise into cylinders. Refrigerate the peppers for 3 hours, tightly wrapped. To serve, slice each roll into 6 slices.

*Note:* The peppers can be stuffed 1 day in advance and refrigerated, tightly covered. Slice the rolls just before serving.

These colorful pinwheels are a wonderful, light hors d'oeuvre. They pair well with wines and appeal to everyone who wants just a small nibble before a large dinner.

*When peeling a large number of peppers of any color, the fastest way to do it is to fry them in hot oil, turning them with tongs until all surfaces have blistered. Then place them in a plastic bag and they will be easy to peel.*

Admittedly, including crushed potato chips in the ingredient list is unusual, but they make these the crunchiest as well as most flavorful cheese crackers you'll ever taste.

*If you're grating cheese by hand, rather than with a food processor, spray the grater with vegetable oil spray and it will be much easier to clean.*

*Good quality Gruyère or Swiss cheese work as well in this recipe as Cheddar.*

# Cheddar Crackers

[ Makes 2 dozen ]

One 5.5-ounce bag potato chips

1 1/2 cups grated sharp Cheddar cheese

5 tablespoons unsalted butter, melted

1/3 cup all-purpose flour

1/2 teaspoon cayenne, or to taste

*1.* Preheat the oven to 350°F.

*2.* Place the potato chips in a food processor fitted with a steel blade. Coarsely chop the chips, pulsing.

*3.* Scrape the potato chip crumbs into a bowl and add the cheese, butter, flour, and cayenne. Stir until the mixture is combined and holds together when pressed in the palm of your hand. Form 1 tablespoon of the mixture into a ball. Place it on an ungreased baking sheet and flatten it into a circle with the bottom of a floured glass or with your fingers. Repeat with the remaining dough, leaving 1 inch between the circles.

*4.* Bake for 15 to 18 minutes, or until browned. Cool the crackers on the baking sheet for 2 minutes, then transfer them to a cooling rack with a spatula to cool completely. Serve at room temperature.

*Note:* The crackers can be made 2 days in advance and kept at room temperature in a tightly sealed container.

# Chicken Satay with Spicy Thai Peanut Sauce

[ Makes 3 dozen ]

| | |
|---|---|
| 4 boneless and skinless chicken breast halves | 2 tablespoons Chinese chili paste |
| 1/2 cup soy sauce | 4 garlic cloves, minced |
| 1/2 cup (firmly packed) dark brown sugar | 1 tablespoon sesame oil |
| 1/4 cup freshly squeezed lime juice | 1 cup Spicy Thai Peanut Sauce (page 175) |

*1.* Trim the fat from the chicken breasts and pull off the tenderloin. Remove the tendon from the center of the tenderloin by holding down the tip with your finger and scraping away the meat with the dull side of paring knife. Cut the tenderloins in half, and cut the remaining chicken meat into 1-inch cubes.

*2.* Combine the soy sauce, brown sugar, lime juice, chili paste, garlic, and sesame oil in a heavy plastic bag and blend well. Add the chicken pieces and marinate, refrigerated, for 3 hours, turning the bag occasionally.

*3.* Light a charcoal or gas grill. Remove the chicken from the marinade and discard the marinade. Grill the chicken pieces for 3 to 5 minutes, turning them with tongs, or until brown and cooked through. Spear each piece of chicken with a toothpick or bamboo skewer and serve hot with a cup of the Spicy Thai Peanut Sauce for dipping.

*Note:* The chicken can marinate for up to 6 hours, and it can be cooked 1 day in advance and refrigerated, tightly covered. Reheat it in a 350°F. oven wrapped in aluminum foil for 5 to 10 minutes, or until hot.

Satays are part of many Asian cultures, and these morsels of spicy chicken are inspired by Thai cooking. Almost any form of protein—from cubes of pork and beef to strips of salmon—can be treated in the same way and will be equally delectable.

*I serve these, as well as other Asian hors d'oeuvres, in a bamboo steamer. I line the steamer with plastic wrap and then with leaves of green or red head lettuce. In addition to placing a cup of sauce in the steamer, I also place a half lime so that people can spear it with used toothpicks.*

*Wash a bamboo steamer quickly and let it dry well before putting it away.*

The balance of aromatic orange and sesame with garlic and ginger create a wonderful yin yang of flavor for these wings, which are also great picnic food. Dishes such as grilled chicken wings are hors d'oeuvres I reserve for parties where plates are being used, since they are a bit messy to eat.

*When removing the zest from citrus fruits wash them first with mild soap and water to remove any insecticides that might be lingering on the fruit.*

*If you freeze fresh ginger once it's peeled, you'll find it easier to grate.*

# Grilled Chinese Chicken Wings
[ Makes 24 ]

| | |
|---|---|
| 1 navel orange | 1/4 cup soy sauce |
| 3 scallions, trimmed and cut into 2-inch sections | 1/4 cup sesame oil |
| 6 garlic cloves, peeled | Freshly ground black pepper to taste |
| 4 slices fresh ginger | 24 chicken wing drumettes |

28

1. Remove the orange zest from the orange with a sharp paring knife. Squeeze the juice out of the orange and set aside.

2. Place the zest, scallions, garlic, and ginger in a food processor fitted with a steel blade. Process until very finely chopped. Scrape the mixture into a heavy plastic bag, add the orange juice, soy sauce, sesame oil, and pepper and mix well. Add the chicken wings. Marinate the chicken wings, refrigerated, for at least 6 hours, preferably overnight, turning the bag occasionally so the wings marinate evenly.

3. Light a charcoal or gas grill.

4. When the fire is medium hot, grill the wings for a total of 10 to 15 minutes, or until cooked through. Serve hot, at room temperature, or chilled.

*Note:* The wings can be grilled 1 day in advance and refrigerated, tightly covered.

# Prosciutto and Cheese Swirls

[ Makes 3 dozen ]

1 cup finely grated Swiss cheese

2 tablespoons chopped fresh rosemary or
   2 teaspoons dried rosemary

Freshly ground black pepper to taste

1/2 pound puff pastry, defrosted if frozen

1 egg, lightly beaten

1/4 pound prosciutto, thinly sliced

*1.* Combine the cheese, rosemary, and pepper in a mixing bowl and set aside. Place the puff pastry sheet on a lightly floured surface. Cut the puff pastry sheet in half horizontally. Set one half aside.
*2.* Brush the far edge of 1 pastry sheet with egg. Arrange half the prosciutto slices on the sheet, stopping before the egg wash. Sprinkle the prosciutto with half the cheese and roll the pastry into a log, starting with the near edge. Press the edges closed and repeat with the second sheet. Chill the logs, seam side down, for at least 3 hours, covered with plastic wrap.
*3.* Preheat the oven to 400°F. Grease 2 baking sheets.
*4.* Cut the logs into slices 1/2 inch thick and arrange them 1 inch apart on the baking sheets. Bake the swirls for 14 to 16 minutes, or until lightly browned. Cool for 2 minutes, then serve immediately.

*Note:* The logs can be prepared 2 days in advance and refrigerated, tightly covered. Do not bake the swirls until just before serving.

29

*These attractive swirls are really very easy to make and they're a perfect choice for a light, crunchy hors d'oeuvre before a heavy dinner.*

*Feel free to experiment with this pinwheel format. Cheddar cheese works well and the prosciutto can be omitted to make these a vegetarian treat.*

*To keep hard cheeses from drying, rub the cut surfaces with butter, and then wrap them with plastic wrap before refrigerating.*

I love the combination of meats in classic Italian sandwiches, and this hearty hors d'oeuvre turns the filling into a grilled cheese sandwich encased in a crispy tortilla. This dish feeds six as a brunch or lunch dish; serve it with a tossed salad or Classic Caesar Salad (page 46).

*The muffuletta sandwich was invented at the Central Grocery in French Quarter of New Orleans almost a century ago, and the name comes from the round Sicilian muffuletta bread on which the meats and cheeses are layered. In addition to the shape, what differentiates the muffuletta from hoagies and submarines from other parts of the country is the olive salad topping.*

## Muffuletta Quesadillas
[ Makes 18 ]

Vegetable oil spray

1 cup pimiento-stuffed green olives

3 garlic cloves, minced

2 tablespoons chopped parsley

1 tablespoon olive oil

1 tablespoon white wine vinegar

Six 6-inch flour tortillas

6 slices mortadella, about 1/4 pound

6 slices baked ham, about 1/4 pound

12 slices Genoa salami, about 1/4 pound

6 slices provolone cheese, about 1/4 pound

30

*1.* Preheat the oven to 450°F. Cover a baking sheet with heavy-duty aluminum foil and spray and foil with vegetable oil spray.

*2.* Place the olives in a food processor fitted with a steel blade. Finely chop, pulsing. Scrape the olives into a small mixing bowl and add the garlic, parsley, olive oil, and vinegar. Stir well and set aside.

*3.* Wrap the tortillas in plastic wrap and microwave on HIGH (100%) for 20 to 30 seconds, or until pliable. Layer the mortadella, ham, salami, and provolone on half of each tortilla. Top with the olive salad. Fold the tortillas over the filling and press them closed with the palm of your hand or with a spatula. Space the quesadillas evenly on the baking sheet and spray the tops with vegetable oil spray.

*4.* Bake the quesadillas for 5 minutes, turn them gently with a spatula, and bake for 5 minutes more, or until browned. Remove them from the oven, allow them to sit for 3 minutes, then cut each into 3 sections and serve.

*Note:* The quesadillas can be assembled 1 day before baking. Refrigerate them separated by layers of plastic wrap.

*31*

# Great from the Start:
## Appetizers & Small Salads

This easy appetizer comes from the New Orleans Creole tradition. The bright flavors and colors from the mélange of marinated vegetables enliven the delicate flavor of the shrimp. This dish works well on a buffet or as part of an antipasto table, too.

*It's best to cook shrimp with the shells on. To keep the shrimp tender, add them to boiling salted water and then turn off the heat. Cover the pan and let the shrimp sit for 5 minutes.*

# Creole Marinated Fresh Shrimp

[ Makes 6 ]

1 1/2 pounds large shrimp, cooked

3/4 cup diced celery

3/4 cup chopped pickled Italian gardiniera vegetables

12 peperoncini, chopped

4 whole canned pimientos or roasted and skinned red peppers

4 garlic cloves, minced

1/2 bunch Italian parsley

1/2 cup white wine vinegar

2 tablespoons freshly squeezed lemon juice

2 tablespoons fresh oregano leaves

Salt and freshly ground black pepper to taste

1/2 cup extra virgin olive oil

3 cups salad greens or 6 large leaves Boston lettuce

*1.* Remove the tails from the shrimp, if necessary, and place the shrimp in a large mixing bowl.

*2.* Chop the celery, gardiniera vegetables, peperoncini, pimientos, garlic, and parsley with a few pulse actions in a food processor fitted with a steel blade. Be careful not to chop the ingredients too fine. Scrape the mixture into the bowl with the shrimp.

*3.* Combine the vinegar, lemon juice, oregano, salt, and pepper in a jar with a tight-fitting lid. Shake vigorously, then add the olive oil and shake again. Add the dressing to the bowl, and mix it with the shrimp and vegetables. Refrigerate for 2 hours.

*4.* To serve, divide the mixed greens or lettuce leaves onto small plates, and mound the shrimp in the center.

*Note:* Both the seafood and vegetable marinade can be prepared up to 1 day in advance and refrigerated, tightly covered. Do not combine them until a few hours before serving time.

# Germaine's Scallop Salad

[ Serves 6 ]

1 1/2 pounds bay scallops, cleaned and rinsed

1 1/2 cups freshly squeezed lemon juice

Freshly ground white pepper to taste

1/4 cup vegetable oil

3 tablespoons distilled white vinegar

2 garlic cloves, minced

1/2 large white onion, chopped

1 tablespoon sugar

1 tablespoon Dijon mustard

1/4 cup chopped dill

Salt to taste

1/4 pound snow peas, stems removed

3 cups shredded iceberg lettuce

6 tablespoons pine nuts

*1.* Combine the scallops, lemon juice, and white pepper in a heavy plastic bag. Marinate refrigerated for at least 4 hours, or overnight.

*2.* In a blender or food processor fitted with a steel blade, combine the oil, vinegar, garlic, onion, sugar, mustard, and half of the dill. Puree until smooth. Refrigerate.

*3.* Place the snow peas in a microwave-safe dish with 2 tablespoons of water. Cover with plastic wrap, and microwave on HIGH (100%) for 45 seconds. Carefully remove the plastic wrap and plunge the snow peas into a bowl of ice water to stop the cooking action. When cold, drain and slice into thin strips.

*4.* To serve, drain the scallops and mix them with the dressing. Arrange the shredded lettuce on plates and spoon some scallops and dressing over it. Garnish each plate with snow peas and sprinkle with the remaining dill and the pine nuts.

*Note:* While the dressing and snow peas can be prepared 2 days in advance and refrigerated, do not allow the scallops to marinate for more than 1 day.

Germaine's, unfortunately now closed, was a pan-Asian restaurant in Washington that was always a stellar choice for any meal. Germaine Swanson is Vietnamese, and this zesty salad—a variation on ceviche—is one of the original fusion dishes, since it uses our succulent Nantucket bay scallops.

*The lemon juice makes the scallops appear and taste cooked, although they remain raw. This process is called acidulation, and it's used extensively in South American cooking.*

If I had to select the food of one continent as the fare for all my meals, it would definitely be Asia. The nuances created with the repertoire of seasonings produces endless variety. Fish with black bean sauce is fairly traditional, but serving these mollusks cold is my improvisation.

*Mussels have a tendency to contain grit, and an easy way to achieve a sand-free dish is to soak the mussels in salted water for 1 hour before cooking them. They will purge themselves of any dirt.*

*While mussels are native to the waters around Nantucket, I prefer the larger ones from New Zealand found in some fish stores.*

# Clams and Mussels with Black Bean Sauce

[ Serves 6 ]

2 dozen littleneck clams

2 dozen large mussels, debearded

2 tablespoons Chinese black beans, coarsely chopped

1/3 cup dry sherry

1 tablespoon Asian sesame oil

1/4 cup thinly sliced scallion rings

4 garlic cloves, peeled and minced

2 tablespoons finely minced ginger

2 tablespoons soy sauce

3 tablespoons thinly sliced scallion rings, for garnish

1. Scrub the clams and mussels well under cold running water. Discard any mollusk that does not shut tightly. Set aside. Stir the black beans into the sherry to plump for 10 minutes.

2. Heat the sesame oil in a large skillet over medium-high heat. Add the 1/4 cup scallions, the garlic, and ginger, and sauté, stirring constantly, for 2 minutes. Add the clams, mussels, sherry mixture, and soy sauce. Cover the pan and bring to a boil over high heat. Steam for 3 minutes, stir to redistribute the seafood, and steam for 3 minutes more. Discard any clams or mussels that did not open and remove the pan from the heat.

3. When cool enough to handle, remove the mollusks and discard the loose shells. Using a paring knife, release the mollusk from the remaining shell. Place the mollusks on a platter, cover tightly with plastic wrap, and refrigerate. Return the pan to the heat and reduce the remaining pan juices by half. Scrape the mixture into a small bowl and refrigerate. Spoon a teaspoon of the mixture onto each mollusk, and sprinkle with remaining 3 tablespoons scallion rings. Serve chilled.

*Note:* The seafood and the topping can be prepared 1 day in advance.

# Baked Clams

[ Serves 4 to 6 ]

5 tablespoons unsalted butter

2 tablespoons minced garlic

3/4 cup finely chopped onion

1 red bell pepper, seeds and ribs removed,
   finely chopped

1/2 green bell pepper, seeds and ribs removed,
   finely chopped

1 1/2 cups Italian seasoned breadcrumbs

1/4 cup grated parmesan cheese

24 cherrystone or littleneck clams, shucked

*1.* Melt the butter in a large skillet over medium heat. Add the garlic and onion and sauté for 3 minutes, stirring frequently. Add the red and green bell peppers and cook, stirring frequently, until the peppers are soft, 5 to 7 minutes.

*2.* Add the breadcrumbs and cheese to the mixture and stir to combine. Set aside.

*3.* Preheat the oven to 425°F.

*4.* Mound the topping on the raw clams, using about 1 tablespoon per clam. Bake for 5 to 8 minutes, depending on the size of the clam, or until the clams are hot and the topping is brown. Serve immediately.

*Note:* The topping can be made up to 2 days in advance and refrigerated in a container or heavy plastic bag.

This variation on Clams Casino is the first recipe I ever devised; it's more than thirty years old and I still love it. The topping keeps the clams tender and adds complex flavors to every bite.

*Here's a trick to open the mollusks quickly. Scrub the clams well under cold running water, discarding any that do not close tightly while being scrubbed. Place the clams in a mixing bowl, and cover them with very hot tap water. In a few minutes the shells should be partially opened. Holding the clam in your hand with the hinge in the crook of your thumb, insert your knife and cut the muscles holding the shells together. Then remove the clam from the shell. Do this process over a mixing bowl to catch the precious clam juice.*

Do-ahead and soufflés are not an oxymoron. These are actually a baked mousse that puffs for a second time when reheated in a sauce. There could be no more elegant appetizer than this one. You can also serve two as a main course for lunch, brunch, or dinner.

# Do-Ahead Lobster Soufflés

[ Serves 8 ]

Lobster Soufflés

1 cup diced lobster meat

1 tablespoon dry sherry

1 cup milk

5 tablespoons all-purpose flour

3 egg yolks

1/2 cup grated Swiss cheese

Salt and freshly ground white pepper to taste

4 egg whites

Pinch of cream of tartar

Lobster Bisque Sauce

1 quart of Lobster Stock (page 62)
 or seafood stock

1 tablespoon unsalted butter

1 tablespoon all-purpose flour

2 teaspoons paprika

2 teaspoons tomato paste

1 teaspoon chopped fresh tarragon or
 pinch of dried tarragon

1 cup half-and-half

Salt and freshly ground black pepper to taste

38

1. To prepare the soufflés, preheat the oven to 375°F. Generously butter 8 individual 6- to 8-ounce custard cups or ramekins and set aside.

2. Sprinkle the lobster meat with the sherry and set aside. Whisk the milk into the flour in a small saucepan and set over medium heat. Whisk constantly as it comes to a boil and thickens. Let it cool briefly, and then transfer the mixture to a food processor fitted with a steel blade. Beat in the egg yolks, one at a time, beating well between each addition. Beat in the cheese, season with salt and pepper, and scrape into a mixing bowl.

3. Place the egg whites in a clean bowl and beat at medium speed with an electric mixer until thick and foamy. Add the cream of tartar and beat on high speed until stiff peaks form. Stir one-fourth of the mixture into the egg yolks to lighten them, then gently fold in the remainder, along with the lobster.

4. Divide the mixture among the prepared cups, and place them in a roasting pan. Place the pan in the oven and pour boiling water into the pan so that it comes halfway up the sides of the cups. Bake for 14 to 18 minutes, or until the soufflés are puffed and lightly brown on the tops.

5. Remove the soufflés from the pan, and allow to cool for 10 minutes; they will fall. Run the tip of a knife around the inside of the cups and invert the soufflés into a buttered ovenproof baking dish.

6. To prepare the lobster sauce, bring the stock to a boil in a small saucepan over high heat. Boil until only 1 cup remains. Pour it into a measuring cup and set aside. Melt the butter in the saucepan over low heat. Stir in the flour and paprika, and cook over low heat, stirring constantly, for 2 minutes. Stir in the tomato paste and tarragon, then whisk in the reduced stock and half-and-half. Bring to a boil and simmer for 2 minutes. Season with salt and pepper.

7. To serve, preheat the oven to 375°F. Pour the sauce around the soufflés, and bake for 12 to 14 minutes. The soufflés will absorb most of the sauce and puff again. Serve immediately.

*Note:* The soufflés and sauce can be prepared up to 1 day in advance and refrigerated, separately, tightly covered. Bring them to room temperature before the second baking.

*For spinach soufflés, substitute 1 package (10 1/2 ounces) frozen chopped spinach for the sherried lobster meat. Prepare the frozen spinach according to package directions, then press it in a colander to remove all water. Bake as directed. Make a simple cheese sauce instead of the lobster bisque sauce.*

In the late 1980s Everett Reid was the chef at American Seasons on Centre Street in Nantucket, and this pancake was one of his signature appetizers. Alas, with the change of ownership it disappeared from the menu, but I took notes on how it was made for my book *Great Chefs of the East*. The pancakes are admittedly a good deal of work; however most of it can be done in advance, and the results are well worth the effort. To serve these as an hors d'oeuvre, form the pancakes with two tablespoons of batter; the recipe will make two dozen.

40

# Everett Reid's Smoked Lobster Pancake

[ Serves 6 ]

1 cup hickory or applewood chips

One 1 1/2-pound live lobster

3 tablespoons unsalted butter

6 tablespoons olive oil

3 cups stemmed wild mushrooms, preferably a mixture of shiitake and chantrelles, cut into 1-inch pieces

Salt and freshly ground black pepper to taste

2 1/4 cups all-purpose flour

1 tablespoon baking powder

2 eggs, lightly beaten

1 3/4 cups milk

6 scallions, trimmed and thinly sliced

6 tablespoons crème fraîche

6 teaspoons salmon or whitefish caviar

*1.* Light a charcoal or gas grill. Soak the wood chips in cold water. Bring a pot of salted water to a boil. Plunge the lobster into the boiling water head first and boil it for 3 minutes. Remove it from the water with tongs and when cool enough to handle, cut off the tail and split it lengthwise down the middle. Break off the claws and crack them open.

*2.* Drain the wood chips and sprinkle them on the hot fire. Place the lobster on the cooking rack and cover the grill. Smoke the lobster for 5 minutes, turn the pieces over, and smoke them for 3 minutes more. Remove the lobster from the grill, remove the meat from the shells, and cut it into 1/2-inch dice. Set aside.

*3.* Heat the butter and 2 tablespoons of the olive oil in a skillet over medium-high heat. Add the mushrooms and sauté, stirring often, for 3 to 5 minutes, or until they are brown and tender. Season the mushrooms with salt and pepper, and set aside.

*4.* Combine the flour and baking powder in a mixing bowl. Whisk the eggs and milk together and whisk the mixture into the dry ingredients. Stir in the scallions and season the batter with salt and pepper.

*5.* Heat the remaining olive oil in a skillet over medium-high heat. Form pancakes with 1/2 cup of the batter and sprinkle each with one sixth of the lobster meat and one sixth of the mushrooms. Fry the pancakes until they are brown on the bottom and the surface is beginning to look dry. Turn the pancakes with a spatula and cook the other side. This may have to be done in 2 batches. Serve immediately, topped with crème fraîche and caviar.

*Note:* The lobster and mushrooms can be cooked 1 day in advance and refrigerated, tightly covered. Do not make the pancake batter or fry the pancakes until just before serving.

*If you're cooking a lobster larger than three pounds, conventional crackers will not be able to break the claws. Place the lobster on a cutting board and pound the edge of a heavy chef's knife into the claw with a hammer. Once the shell has cracked, turn the lobster over and crack the other side. The top of the shell will slip right off, so removing the claw meat is easy.*

There's no trick to making sausage yourself; it involves nothing more than seasoning meat. In this case, the spicy lamb tops salad greens and the simple honey mustard dressing complements both. Double the recipe, and it will serve six as an entree.

*I use the same seasoning for ground lamb to be grilled as lamb burgers and placed on buns at a barbecue.*

*I've found that some people shy away from lamb. If you're one of them, try this recipe with a combination of ground beef and ground pork.*

# Grilled Lamb Sausage Salad

[ Serves 6 ]

2 pounds lean ground lamb

4 garlic cloves, minced

1 tablespoon chili powder

1 teaspoon ground fennel seeds, ground

1 teaspoon ground cumin

1/2 teaspoon cayenne

Salt to taste

1/2 cup Dijon mustard

1/3 cup honey

3 cups mixed salad greens

42

*1.* Light a charcoal or gas grill. Combine the lamb with the garlic, chili powder, fennel seeds, cumin, cayenne, and salt. Form the mixture into 12 patties 1/2 inch thick.

*2.* To prepare the dressing, combine the mustard and honey. Broil the patties for 3 minutes on each side, or until medium rare.

*3.* To serve, toss the greens with a little of the dressing and place 2 patties on a plate with a dollop of dressing and some greens. Serve immediately.

*Note:* The patties and sauce can be made 1 day in advance and refrigerated, covered with plastic wrap. Do not grill the meat or toss the salad until just before serving.

# Grilled Corn and Sausage Salad

[ Serves 6 ]

1 cup mesquite chips

4 ears of fresh corn, unshucked

3/4 pound bulk pork sausage

1/2 cup finely chopped red bell pepper

1/2 cup finely chopped green bell pepper

3 scallions, white parts and 2-inches of the
 green tops, finely chopped,

3 tablespoons extra virgin olive oil

2 tablespoons freshly squeezed lime juice

2 tablespoons pure maple syrup

Salt and freshly ground black pepper to taste

3 tablespoons finely chopped cilantro

*1.* Light a charcoal or gas grill and soak the mesquite chips in cold water to cover for 15 minutes.

*2.* Remove all but 1 layer of the husks from the corn and pull out the corn silks. Soak the corn in cold water to cover for 10 minutes. Drain the mesquite chips and place on the fire. Grill the corn for 10 to 15 minutes, turning with tongs occasionally.

*3.* When cool enough to handle, discard the husks, and cut the kernels off the cobs, using a sharp serrated knife.

*4.* Cook the sausage in a frying pan over medium heat, breaking up lumps with a fork. Cook until brown. Combine the sausage and its fat with the corn, red and green bell peppers, and scallions in a mixing bowl. Combine the olive oil, lime juice, maple syrup, and salt and pepper in a jar with a tight-fitting lid. Shake well, and toss with the corn mixture. Toss with the cilantro and serve at room temperature.

*Note:* The salad can be made up to 2 days in advance and refrigerated, tightly covered with plastic wrap. Allow it to sit at room temperature for a few hours to take the chill off. Do not add the cilantro until just before serving.

It's not an August meal at my table if fresh corn in some form isn't part of it, and this salad is an especially appetizing way to prepare it. The sausage and simple dressing enhance the flavor of grilled corn. You can also serve this as a side dish with grilled meats or poultry.

*Humorist Garrison Keillor once quipped that "sex is good, but not as good as fresh, sweet corn."*

This salad is versatile; it can be served at brunches as well as dinners. The soft, creamy eggs soften the peppery sharpness of the arugula, and the bacon adds a hearty, smoky accent flavor.

*An alternative to frying bacon is to bake it in a 325°F. oven until crisp. The length of time will depend on the thickness of the bacon.*

# Bacon, Egg, and Arugula Salad
[ Serves 6 ]

3/4 pound bacon

2 tablespoons unsalted butter

10 eggs

1/3 cup sour cream

Salt and freshly ground black pepper to taste

6 cups arugula leaves, rinsed, stems removed

1/3 cup Balsamic Vinaigrette (page 170)

*1.* Cook the bacon in a large skillet until crisp. Drain and crumble the bacon. Set aside. Pour the bacon grease out of the skillet.

*2.* Melt the butter in the same skillet over low heat. Whisk the eggs with the sour cream and salt and pepper. When the butter has melted, add the eggs to the pan, then cover the pan. After 3 minutes, stir the eggs and cover the pan again. Cook until the eggs are three quarters set.

*3.* While the eggs are cooking, place the arugula in a salad bowl. Toss with the vinaigrette. Add the reserved bacon and hot eggs to the salad bowl, and toss gently. Serve immediately.

*Note:* The Balsamic Vinaigrette can be made 2 days in advance and refrigerated, tightly covered.

# Tomato and Mozzarella with Oregano

[ Serves 6 ]

2 pints cherry tomatoes, rinsed, stemmed, and halved

Salt and freshly ground black pepper to taste

1 pound fresh mozzarella cheese, cut into 1/2-inch dice

3 tablespoons chopped oregano

2 tablespoons capers, rinsed

1/4 cup balsamic vinegar

1/4 cup extra virgin olive oil

*1.* Place the cherry tomatoes in a mixing bowl and sprinkle them with salt and pepper. Refrigerate for 30 minutes. Drain the tomatoes, and place them in a mixing bowl.

*2.* Add the mozzarella, oregano, and capers to the tomatoes. Sprinkle the salad with the vinegar and oil, and toss well. Serve immediately.

*Note:* The salad can be made 4 hours in advance and refrigerated, tightly covered.

*This version of the classic Italian salad is easier to serve since it does not have to be meticulously layered. The zesty capers and aromatic oregano are surprising alternatives to traditional basil.*

*Capers are the preserved flower buds of a bushy plant that grows near the Mediterranean; they are never eaten fresh. They are always salted or pickled.*

There are a million bland, creamy dressings around passing themselves off as Caesar dressing. This one, laced with garlic and anchovy paste, is close to the original. To turn this salad into a full meal, top it with slices of grilled chicken breast, shrimp, or salmon.

*Caesar Salad has nothing to do with Rome. It was the invention of Caesar Cardini, who owned a restaurant in Tijuana, Mexico. The salad caught on with his Hollywood patrons and became popularized at such Los Angeles bastions as Chasen's.*

# Classic Caesar Salad

[ Serves 6 ]

**Caesar Dressing**

1 egg

One 2-ounce tube anchovy paste

5 garlic cloves, minced

1/4 cup freshly squeezed lemon juice

2 tablespoons Dijon mustard

1/2 cup extra virgin olive oil

**Caesar Salad**

24 leaves romaine lettuce, cleaned and broken into 1 1/2-inch pieces

1/2 cup freshly grated parmesan cheese

1 1/2 cups croutons, preferably homemade

6 to 12 anchovy fillets

Freshly ground black pepper to taste

*1.* To prepare the dressing, bring a small saucepan of water to a boil over high heat. Add the egg and boil for 1 minute. Remove the egg from the water with a slotted spoon and break it into a jar with a tight-fitting lid, scraping the inside of the shell. Add the anchovy paste, garlic, lemon juice, and mustard and shake well. Add the olive oil and shake well again. Season with pepper and set aside.

*2.* To prepare the salad, toss the lettuce with the parmesan, croutons, and enough dressing to coat lightly. Divide the salad among 6 plates and top each portion with anchovies and pepper. Serve immediately.

*Note:* The dressing can be made 1 day in advance and refrigerated, tightly covered.

## Fennel Salad

[ Serves 6 ]

2 fennel bulbs, well chilled

1/4 cup finely chopped parsley

1/3 cup fruity olive oil

3 tablespoons freshly squeezed lemon juice

2 teaspoons anchovy paste or 1/2 teaspoon salt

2 garlic cloves, minced

Freshly ground black pepper to taste

1. Trim the stalks and root ends from the fennel bulbs. Using a thin slicing disk of a food processor, slice the fennel. This can also be done on a mandoline or with a very sharp knife. Place the fennel in a salad bowl and toss with the parsley.

2. Place the olive oil, lemon juice, anchovy paste, garlic, and pepper in a jar with a tight-fitting lid and shake well. Toss the dressing with the fennel and serve immediately.

*Note:* The salad can be prepared 3 hours in advance and refrigerated, tightly covered.

*Anise-flavored fresh fennel is the star of this crunchy salad drawn from classic Italian cooking. It goes especially well with grilled fish and seafood.*

*Fennel is best from August to May. The bulbs should be compact, clean, and bright white or very pale green. Avoid dry-looking bulbs, bulbs with brown spots, or a spreading bulb, which may be overly mature and have a woody texture.*

*While the salad uses the bulb of the fennel, save the stalks and use them as an alternative to celery in chicken and tuna salad.*

# The Brilliant Bowl:

## Soups for All Seasons

This chilly fruity soup is pale green and luscious, with just a hint of mint. If you use yogurt, it is also an excellent diet dish that is very low in calories. I take it to the beach on hot days, and it's a wonderful start to any meal on a hot, steamy summer day.

*Barbara Streisand is reported to have said that "success to me is having ten honeydew melons and eating only the top half of each one."*

# Honeydew Gazpacho

[ Serves 6 ]

1 ripe honeydew melon, peeled, seeded, and diced

2 cups sliced celery

2 cucumbers, peeled, seeded, and diced

1 cup sour cream or non-fat yogurt

1/3 cup white wine vinegar

3 tablespoons chopped fresh mint

Salt and freshly ground white pepper to taste

50

*1.* Combine the melon, celery, onion, cucumber, sour cream, vinegar and mint in a food processor fitted with a steel blade or in a blender. Puree until smooth, and season with salt and pepper to taste. *2.* Refrigerate until cold, and serve.

*Note:* The soup can be prepared up to 1 day in advance.

# Gazpacho

[ Serves 6 to 8 ]

1 medium Bermuda or other sweet white
   onion, peeled and quartered

1 medium cucumber, peeled, seeded,
   and cut into 1-inch sections

1/2 green bell pepper, seeds and ribs
   removed, diced

1/2 red bell pepper, seeds and ribs
   removed, diced

3 medium to large ripe tomatoes,
   seeded and diced

3 large garlic cloves, peeled

1 1/2 cups tomato juice

1/4 cup extra virgin olive oil

1 jalapeño or serrano pepper, seeds
   and ribs removed

2 tablespoons balsamic vinegar

2 tablespoons sherry vinegar

1/4 cup chopped cilantro

Salt and freshly ground black pepper to taste

*It* wouldn't be summer without a vat of this Spanish soup in my refrigerator. My version is spicy and contains some mellow vinegars to balance the innate sweetness of the tomatoes. I keep the soup rather chunky and rustic, but if you prefer a smoother texture, just keep the food processor running longer.

*For a brunch eye-opener, add some vodka or gin to a glass of Gazpacho and serve Gazpacho Marys.*

*There's an old Spanish proverb: "Of soup and love, the first is best."*

*1.* Finely chop the onion, cucumber, green pepper, red pepper, and 1 tomato in a food processor. Scrape the mixture into a large bowl.

*2.* Puree the remaining tomatoes with the garlic, tomato juice, olive oil, jalapeño, balsamic vinegar, and sherry vinegar. Stir the puree into the vegetables, add the cilantro, and season with salt and pepper. Chill well.

*Note:* The soup can be made up to 2 days in advance and refrigerated, tightly covered.

Clam Chowder is a year-round soup on the island, and there are as many versions of chowder as there are cooks – all of whom tout theirs as the best. Mine is on the light side, and the broth is enlivened with fresh herbs as well as celery.

*Early chowder recipes call for everything from beer to ketchup, but not milk. What we know as New England chowder dates from the mid-19th century.*

## Nantucket Clam Chowder

[ Serves 4 to 6 ]

1 pint fresh chopped clams
    (or three 6-1/2 ounce cans)

4 tablespoons unsalted butter

2 medium onions, peeled and diced

2 celery stalks, sliced

2 garlic cloves, minced

One 8-ounce bottle clam juice

2 medium redskin potatoes, scrubbed
    and cut into 1/2-inch dice

2 tablespoons chopped parsley

1 bay leaf

1 tablespoon fresh thyme or 1 teaspoon
    dried thyme

Salt and freshly ground black pepper to taste

3 tablespoons all-purpose flour

1 pint milk

1/2 pint heavy cream or half-and-half

1. Drain the clams in a sieve, reserving the juice in a bowl below. Press down with the back of a spoon to extract as much liquid as possible from the clams.

2. Melt 2 tablespoons of the butter in a large saucepan over medium heat. Add the onions, celery, and garlic, and sauté, stirring frequently, for 3 minutes, or until the onions are translucent. Add the clam juice, and reserved clam juice to the pan, along with the potatoes, parsley, bay leaf, thyme, salt and pepper. Bring to a boil, and simmer, covered, for 12 minutes, or until the potatoes are tender.

3. While the mixture is simmering, melt the remaining butter in a small saucepan over low heat. Stir in the flour, and stir constantly for 2 minutes. Raise the heat to medium, and whisk in the milk. Bring to a boil, whisking frequently, and simmer for 2 minutes.

4. Stir the thickened milk into the pot with the vegetables and add the cream and clams. Bring to a boil, and simmer, uncovered, for 3 minutes. Discard the bay leaf, adjust the seasoning, and serve.

*Note:* The chowder can be made up to 2 days in advance and refrigerated, tightly covered. Reheat over low heat, stirring frequently.

*In Melville's* **Moby Dick,** *Ishmael and Queequeg land on Nantucket and are sent to Hosea Hussey's Try Pots; the name comes from the black iron cauldron used aboard whaleships for melting blubber to liquid oil. Melville writes that "fishiest of all fishy places was the Try Pots. Chowder for breakfast, and chowder for dinner, and chowder for supper."*

*Clementine Paddleford was a flowery New York restaurant critic. She once wrote that "chowder breathes reassurance. It steams consolation."*

Lobster Bisque, drawn from classic French cuisine, is an elegant first course for any meal. While the actual recipe is very simple, the key to its flavor is a rich stock made from the bodies and shells of lobsters.

*Never throw out a lobster body. Break the shells into small pieces and freeze them. When you have a half dozen or so, make a batch of stock. Shrimp shells are a good addition to the stock, however fish skin and bones will overpower the flavor of the delicate crustaceans.*

# Lobster Bisque

[ Serves 6 ]

4 quarts Lobster Stock (page 62)

1 onion, peeled and sliced

1 head of garlic, cut in half crosswise

3 tomatoes, seeded and diced

2 tablespoons fresh tarragon or 1 teaspoon dried tarragon

1 tablespoon fresh thyme or 1/2 teaspoon dried thyme

3 sprigs parsley

3/4 cup dry sherry

3 tablespoons unsalted butter

1/4 cup all-purpose flour

1 tablespoon paprika

1 tablespoon tomato paste

2 cups half–and–half

1/2 pound lobster meat, finely diced

Salt and freshly ground black pepper to taste

*1.* Combine the lobster stock with the onion, garlic, tomatoes, tarragon, thyme, parsley, and 1/2 cup of the sherry in a large saucepan. Bring to a boil over high heat, reduce the heat to medium, and boil until the liquid has reduced to 1 quart. Strain the stock, pushing on the solids with the back of a spoon to extract as much liquid as possible. Discard the solids, and set the liquid aside.
*2.* Melt the butter in a saucepan over low heat. Stir in the flour and paprika and cook, stirring constantly, for 2 minutes. Stir in the tomato paste, and then whisk in the reserved lobster stock. Cook over medium heat until the liquid comes to a boil, add the reserved 1/4 cup sherry, and simmer for 3 minutes. Add the half-and-half and simmer for 2 minutes. Add the lobster, season with salt and pepper, and serve.

*Note:* The bisque can be made up to 2 days in advance and refrigerated, tightly covered. Reheat over low heat, stirring frequently.

# Cream of Asparagus Soup

[ Serves 6 ]

2 pounds fresh asparagus

1 quart Chicken Stock (page 63)

5 tablespoons unsalted butter

3 tablespoons all-purpose flour

1 1/2 cups milk

Salt and freshly ground black pepper to taste

*1.* Cut off and discard the bottom 1/2 inch of the asparagus spears. Break the spears to separate the woody ends from the tender stalks. Coarsely chop the woody ends and combine them with the stock in a saucepan. Bring to a boil over high heat, reduce the heat to low, and simmer the stock, partially covered, for 20 minutes. Strain the stock, pushing with the back of a spoon to extract as much liquid as possible. Discard the asparagus ends and set the stock aside.

*2.* While the stock is simmering, heat 2 tablespoons of the butter in a skillet over low heat. Thinly slice the asparagus stalks and add them to the pan. Stir to coat the pieces, sprinkle with salt and pepper, and cook the asparagus, covered, for 10 to 15 minutes, or until the pieces are tender. Puree half the asparagus in a food processor fitted with a steel blade and set aside.

*3.* Melt the remaining 3 tablespoons of butter in a saucepan over low heat. Stir in the flour and cook over low heat, stirring constantly, for 2 minutes. Raise the heat to medium-high and whisk in the stock. Bring to a boil and add the milk, pureed asparagus, and remaining asparagus pieces. Simmer the soup over low heat for 5 minutes, stirring occasionally. Season the soup with salt and pepper and serve hot.

*Note:* The soup can be prepared 2 days in advance and refrigerated, tightly covered. Reheat it over low heat, stirring occasionally.

*This creamy soup is the essence of spring, and the grassy asparagus flavor is strengthened by simmering the stalk ends that would normally be discarded.*

*The ancient Egyptians cultivated asparagus and found it a worthy offering to their gods.*

*Look for asparagus with rich green color. The freshest asparagus has firm, straight stalks and closed, compact tips. Its appearance should be crisp and firm, not limp or wrinkled. For ease of cooking, it's best to select stalks of the same diameter.*

*It* never occurred to me that sweet red bell pepper could be a soup star until I enjoyed a soup similar to this one at Patrick O'Connell's famed Inn at Little Washington in Virginia's Shenandoah Mountains.

*Orange or yellow peppers can be substituted for the red peppers in this recipe, but don't try it with green peppers. Green peppers are immature red peppers, and the flavor will be too bitter.*

## Red Pepper Bisque

[ Serves 6 ]

2 tablespoons unsalted butter

1 medium onion, peeled and chopped

4 red bell peppers, seeds and ribs removed, diced

3 garlic cloves, minced

1 jalapeño chili, seeds and ribs removed, diced

1 tablespoon fennel seeds

1/4 cup all-purpose flour

4 cups Chicken Stock (page 63)

1 tablespoon tomato paste

1 tablespoon fresh thyme or 1 teaspoon dried thyme

1 bay leaf

1 cup heavy cream

Salt and freshly ground black pepper to taste

56

*1.* Melt the butter in a saucepan over medium heat. Add the onion, red peppers, garlic, jalapeño, and fennel seed. Sauté, stirring frequently, for 3 minutes, or until the onion is translucent. Reduce the heat to low, stir in the flour, and cook, stirring constantly, for 2 minutes. Raise the heat to medium, and whisk in the stock and tomato paste. Bring to a boil, add the thyme and bay leaf, reduce the heat to low, and simmer, partially covered, for 30 minutes.

*2.* Remove the bay leaf and puree the soup in a food processor fitted with a steel blade or in a blender. Return the soup to the saucepan, and add the cream. Bring to a boil over medium heat, reduce the heat, and simmer for 3 minutes. Season with salt and pepper and serve.

*Note:* The soup can be prepared up to 2 days in advance and refrigerated, tightly covered. Reheat it over low heat.

# Greek Lemon Egg Soup

[ Serves 6 ]

7 cups Chicken Stock (page 63)

2/3 cup orzo

4 eggs

1/3 cup freshly squeezed lemon juice

1/2 teaspoon grated lemon zest

Salt and freshly ground white pepper to taste

1. Bring the stock to a boil in a saucepan. Add the orzo and simmer, covered, for 10 to 15 minutes, or until the orzo is tender. The time depends on the brand of orzo used.

2. While the stock is simmering, whisk the eggs well with the lemon juice and lemon zest. When the orzo is tender, remove the pan from the heat, and stir for 45 seconds to cool the soup; the liquid should not be bubbling or simmering at all.

3. Stir in the egg mixture, cover the pan, and let the soup sit for 5 minutes to thicken. Serve immediately.

*Note:* Long grain rice can be substituted for orzo. Simmer the rice for 15 to 20 minutes, or until soft. The soup can be prepared 1 day in advance and refrigerated, tightly covered. Reheat it over very low heat, stirring frequently, to ensure that the eggs do not scramble.

This soup, called *avgolemono*, is part of classic Greek cooking. It's thick while not too rich, and it's a perfect starter for heartier foods such as lamb or beef. The key to its flavor is a good chicken stock.

*It's not surprising that this soup is a standard in the Mediterranean, since lemons appear in ancient Greek and Roman murals. It was the Romans who introduced the citrus fruit to both Spain and North Africa, where lemon is still a dominant flavor in many dishes.*

*It's easier to remove the zest from citrus fruits before the juice is extracted. Remove all the zest, not just the amount specified in a recipe, and store it refrigerated in a small plastic bag.*

I love this soup so much that I grill dozens of ears of corn when it's in season and then freeze the kernels. Grilling adds a smoky undertaste to this thick soup, and the corn flavor is reinforced by cornmeal.

*Lewis Carroll wrote: "Beautiful soup! Who cares for fish, game, or any other dish? Who would not give all else for two pennyworth only of beautiful soup?"*

# Grilled Corn Soup

[ Serves 6 to 8 ]

1 cup mesquite chips

8 to 10 medium ears of fresh corn, unshucked

2 tablespoons unsalted butter

4 large garlic cloves, roasted in a 350ºF. oven for 15 minutes and peeled

1/4 cup yellow cornmeal

One 4-ounce can mild green chilies, drained

2 cups Chicken Stock (page 63)

2 cups milk

Salt and freshly ground black pepper to taste

*1.* Light a charcoal or gas grill, and soak the mesquite chips in cold water to cover for 30 minutes.

*2.* Remove all but 1 layer of the husks from the corn, and pull out the corn silks. Soak the corn in cold water to cover for 10 minutes.

*3.* Drain the mesquite chips and place on the fire. Grill the corn for 10 to 15 minutes, turning with tongs occasionally.

*4.* When cool enough to handle, discard the husks, and cut the kernels off the cobs using a sharp serrated knife.

*5.* Melt the butter in a large saucepan, and sauté the kernels over low heat for 5 minutes. Remove 1 cup of kernels, and set aside. Puree the remaining corn, roasted garlic, cornmeal, chilies, and stock in a food processor fitted with a steel blade or in a blender. This will probably have to be done in a few batches. Combine the puree with the milk and heat to a boil over medium heat. Add the reserved corn kernels, and season with salt and pepper to taste. Simmer for 5 minutes over low heat, stirring occasionally.

*Note:* The soup can be made up to 2 days in advance and reheated slowly, but do not let it boil or reduce. After it has been chilled, it may have to be thinned with a little additional milk or stock.

# Classic Onion Soup

[ Serves 6 to 8 ]

3 tablespoons unsalted butter

1 tablespoon olive oil

3 pounds yellow onions, peeled and thinly sliced

1/2 teaspoon salt

1 teaspoon sugar

3 tablespoons all-purpose flour

2 quarts beef, veal, or Chicken Stock (page 63)

3/4 cup dry red wine

1 bay leaf

1 tablespoon fresh thyme or
  1 teaspoon dried thyme

3 tablespoons chopped parsley

Salt and freshly ground black pepper to taste

6 to 8 slices of French bread, cut 1/2 inch thick

1/4 cup freshly grated parmesan cheese

1 to 2 cups grated Gruyère or Swiss cheese

*1.* Heat the butter and oil in a large saucepan over low heat. Add the onions, toss to coat with the fat, and cover the pan. Cook over low heat for 10 minutes, stirring occasionally. Uncover the pan, raise the heat to medium, and stir in the salt and sugar. Cook for 30 to 40 minutes, stirring frequently, until the onions have turned dark brown. If the onions stick to the pan, stir to incorporate the browned juices into the onions.
*2.* Reduce the heat to low, stir in the flour and cook for 2 minutes, stirring constantly. Stir in the stock, wine, bay leaf, thyme, and parsley. Bring the soup to a boil and simmer, partially covered, for 40 minutes. Season with salt and pepper and discard the bay leaf.
*3.* While the soup is simmering, preheat the oven to 400° F.
*4.* Place the slices of bread on a baking sheet, and sprinkle with the parmesan cheese. Bake for 7 to 10 minutes, or until the croutons are brown.
*5.* To serve, ladle the soup into ovenproof bowls. Top each serving with a crouton and some cheese. Place under the broiler until the cheese is melted and brown. Serve immediately.
*Note:* The soup can be made up to 4 days in advance and refrigerated. Reheat it over medium heat until boiling, then top with the crouton and cheese.

There's nothing like a steaming bowl of onion soup topped with a bubbly layer of gooey cheese to warm your body on a winter night. The addition of red wine to the stock deepens the color of the soup as well as enhancing its flavor.

*Out of all the ways I've read to lessen the tear factor of slicing onions, the best one I know is to chill them well in advance.*

This colorful, thick and luscious soup is one of the treats of winter, and the way I traditionally begin Thanksgiving dinner. The innately sweet flavor of the squash is complemented by the spices.

*When choosing acorn or butternut squash, pick one heavy for its size with no blemishes on the skin. These squash are hard to cut; you'll need a sturdy thick knife. They become a bit easier to cut if microwaved on HIGH (100%) for two minutes first. Pierce the skin with a meat fork before cooking them.*

# Cream of Acorn Squash Soup

[ Serves 6 to 8 ]

3 1/2 pounds acorn squash (2 medium) or butternut squash

2 cups Chicken Stock (page 63)

2 tablespoons chopped parsley

1 tablespoon chopped fresh marjoram

1 1/2 cups half-and-half

2 tablespoons molasses

2 tablespoons bourbon

1/4 teaspoon ground cinnamon

Pinch of ground nutmeg

Salt and freshly ground white pepper to taste

1. Preheat the oven to 350° F.
2. Bake the squash on a baking sheet for 1 hour, or until the flesh is tender when probed with a sharp meat fork, turning occasionally during baking. Cut the squash in half, scrape out and discard the seeds, and scrape the flesh from the shell. Cut the flesh into 2-inch chunks.
3. Combine the squash, stock, parsley, and marjoram in a saucepan. Bring to a boil over medium heat, and simmer, partially covered, for 10 minutes.
4. Puree the soup in a blender or food processor fitted with a steel blade. Return it to the pot, and add the half-and-half, molasses, bourbon, cinnamon, nutmeg, and salt and pepper. Bring to a boil over medium heat, stirring frequently, and simmer over low heat for 5 minutes. Serve immediately.

*Note:* Butternut squash can be substituted for the acorn, baking it in the same manner. The soup can be made up to 3 days in advance and reheated over low heat.

# White Bean Soup with Rosemary and Spinach

[ Serves 6 to 8 ]

3/4 pound dried cannellini or
  navy beans, rinsed

2 tablespoons olive oil

1 cup diced onion

1 carrot, peeled and sliced

1 celery stalk, sliced

4 garlic cloves, peeled

1/2 cup diced country ham or prosciutto

2 tablespoons chopped fresh rosemary
  or 2 teaspoons dried rosemary

8 cups Chicken Stock (page 63)

2 cups spinach leaves, stems removed

Salt and freshly ground black pepper to taste

1. Place the beans in a large saucepan, add cold water to cover them by 2 inches, and bring to a boil over high heat. Boil 1 minute. Cover the pan and let the beans soak for 1 hour. Drain the beans.
2. Heat the oil in a large saucepan over medium heat. Add the onion, carrot, celery, garlic, and ham. Sauté, stirring frequently, for 5 minutes. Add the beans, rosemary, and stock and bring to a boil. Simmer, covered, for 30 minutes. Taste the cooking liquid and add enough salt so that it becomes slightly salty. The amount needed will depend on the type of ham used for seasoning.
3. Recover the pot and simmer for 40 to 60 minutes, or until the beans are soft. Puree the mixture in a food processor fitted with the steel blade or in a blender. Return the soup to the pan, and bring to a boil. Add the spinach leaves, and simmer for 2 minutes. Serve hot.

Note: The soup can be made up to 3 days in advance and refrigerated, tightly covered. It will probably thicken from the starch in the beans, but it can be thinned to the desired consistency with some stock when reheated.

On a chilly evening, there is nothing as warming as a bowl of this aromatic, thick, and colorful soup. In fact, with a tossed salad and some crusty garlic bread it can be a meal in itself. The slightly smoky taste from the ham adds depth of flavor.

*When cooking dried beans, always pick them over carefully to remove any pebbles or debris that are frequently included when they're packaged.*

Lobster stock forms the basis for many great fish and seafood stews, and it's essential for dishes like Lobster Bisque (page 54).

*Many good fish stores around the country sell lobster meat that is already cooked and shelled. If you can find one, it's likely to sell you the lobster bodies at a very reasonable price.*

# Lobster Stock

[ Makes 2 quarts ]

6 to 8 lobster bodies

4 quarts water

1 cup dry white wine

1 onion, peeled and quartered

2 carrots, trimmed, scrubbed, and sliced into chunks

2 celery stalks, rinsed and sliced into chunks

6 garlic cloves, peeled

6 sprigs of thyme or 1 1/2 teaspoons dried thyme

4 sprigs of parsley

1 bay leaf

12 black peppercorns

1. Remove the outer shells from the lobster bodies and discard the gills. Break the body in half and discard the sand sac located at the head. Break off the small legs, then break each into pieces. Break the body into pieces.

2. Place the lobster in a large stockpot with the remaining ingredients and bring to a boil over high heat. Reduce the heat to low and simmer the stock for 2 1/2 to 3 hours, or until it is reduced by half. Strain the stock, pressing down on the solids to extract as much liquid as possible. Pour the stock into containers and refrigerate.

*Note:* Lobster stock can be made up to 4 days in advance and kept refrigerated, or it can be frozen for up to 6 months.

# Chicken Stock

[ Makes 3 quarts ]

6 quarts water

5 pounds chicken bones, skin, and trimmings

4 celery stalks, rinsed and cut into thick slices

2 onions, trimmed and quartered

2 carrots, trimmed, scrubbed, and
    cut into thick slices

12 black peppercorns

6 garlic cloves, peeled

4 sprigs of parsley

4 sprigs of thyme or 1 teaspoon dried thyme

2 bay leaves

*1.* Place the water and chicken in a large stockpot, and bring to a boil over high heat. Reduce the heat to a simmer and skim off the foam that rises during the first 10 to 15 minutes of simmering. Simmer for 1 hour, add the remaining ingredients, and simmer for 2 1/2 hours.

*2.* Strain the stock through a fine-meshed sieve and let it cool. Cover and refrigerate. Remove and discard the layer of fat from the surface, spoon the stock into smaller containers, and refrigerate.

*Note:* The stock can be refrigerated and used within 3 days, or it can be frozen for up to 6 months.

Richly flavored, homemade chicken stock is as important as good olive oil in my kitchen. Once you've gotten into the habit of "keeping stocked," you'll appreciate the difference that it makes in all soups and sauces. And making it is as easy as boiling water.

*I never buy chicken to make stock, since there are always scraps left over from cooking chicken. Keep a plastic bag in your freezer for the skin and other tidbits that are trimmed off chicken before it's cooked. When the bag is full, it's time to make stock.*

# One If By Land:
## Poultry & Meat Entrees

This is a hearty entree salad. Cooking the rice in Bloody Mary mix is an easy way to achieve vivid flavor as well as color, and this is a one-dish meal that just needs a green salad.

## Jambalaya Salad

[ Serves 6 ]

Jambalaya Salad

2 cups Bloody Mary mix

1 tablespoon fresh thyme or 1/2 teaspoon dried thyme

1 cup long-grain rice

One 10-ounce package frozen peas

1/2 pound cooked shrimp, peeled, deveined, and cut in half lengthwise

3 cooked boneless and skinless chicken breasts, cut into 1/2-inch dice

1/4 pound baked ham, cut into 1/2-inch dice

6 scallions, trimmed and thinly sliced

2 celery stalks, trimmed and thinly sliced

1/2 red bell pepper, seeds and ribs removed, chopped

Dressing

1/4 cup freshly squeezed lemon juice

3 garlic cloves, minced

Salt and cayenne to taste

1/4 cup olive oil

1. To prepare the salad, bring the Bloody Mary mix and thyme to a boil in a saucepan over high heat. Add the rice, reduce the heat to low, and cook the rice, covered, for 15 to 20 minutes, or until soft. Spread the hot rice on a baking sheet and chill well.

2. While the rice is cooking, cook the peas according to package directions. Drain and chill well.

3. Place the rice and peas in a large bowl and add the shrimp, chicken, ham, scallions, celery, and red pepper.

4. To prepare the dressing, combine the lemon juice, garlic, and salt and cayenne in a jar with a tight-fitting lid and shake well. Add the olive oil and shake well again.

5. Toss the dressing with the salad and serve chilled.

*Note:* The salad and dressing can be prepared 1 day in advance and refrigerated, tightly covered. Do not toss the salad with the dressing until ready to serve.

*Jambalaya is native to the Louisiana bayous, and many experts believe that the name comes from the Spanish word for ham, jamón.*

67

*Tangy* dried currents and succulent dried apricots meld with traditional Moroccan spices and add textural interest to the light couscous base of this toothsome chicken salad. It's refreshing on a summer day.

# Moroccan Chicken Salad

[ Serves 6 ]

## Orange Dressing

1/2 cup freshly squeezed orange juice

2 tablespoons balsamic vinegar

1/4 cup chopped cilantro

4 garlic cloves, minced

1 tablespoon ground cumin

1 teaspoon grated orange zest

Salt and freshly ground black pepper to taste

1/4 cup olive oil

## Couscous Salad

4 1/2 cups water

Two 10-ounce boxes plain couscous

1/2 cup dried currants

1/2 cup chopped dried apricots

4 cooked boneless and skinless chicken breasts, cut into 1/2-inch dice

One 15-ounce can garbanzo beans, drained and rinsed

1/4 pound kalamata olives, pitted and chopped

1 small red onion, peeled and diced

1/2 small fennel bulb, trimmed and diced

*1.* To prepare the dressing, combine the orange juice, vinegar, cilantro, garlic, cumin, orange zest, and salt and pepper in a jar with a tight-fitting lid. Shake well. Add the olive oil and shake well again. Set aside.

*2.* To prepare the couscous, bring the water to a boil in a saucepan over high heat. Add the couscous, currants, and apricots. Cover the pan, turn off the heat, and let the couscous stand for 10 minutes. Fluff the mixture with a fork and transfer it to a mixing bowl. Chill well.

*3.* Add the chicken, beans, olives, onion, and fennel to the couscous. Pour the dressing over the salad, and toss well. Serve chilled.

*Note:* The salad can be prepared 1 day in advance and kept refrigerated, tightly covered.

*This is a recipe that can be personalized in many ways. I sometimes omit the chicken and serve the vegetable couscous as a side dish. Cubes of cooked fish can also be substituted for the chicken.*

69

This is my variation on the famous French dish, Chicken with Forty Cloves of Garlic. The garlic becomes sweet and mellow when braised in the lemony sauce.

*Famed French gastronome Brillat-Savarin wrote that "poultry is for the cook what canvas is for the painter."*

*The easiest way to break apart a whole head of garlic is to slam the root end onto a counter. It should then separate easily.*

# Chicken with Garlic and Lemon

[ Serves 4 ]

1 frying chicken, cut into serving pieces

1/4 cup olive oil

3 heads of garlic, separated into cloves but not peeled

1/3 cup freshly squeezed lemon juice

2 cups Chicken Stock (page 63)

Salt and freshly ground black pepper to taste

2 teaspoons cornstarch mixed with 2 tablespoons cold water

70

1. Preheat the oven to 400°F.

2. Rinse the chicken pieces, and pat dry on paper towels. Heat the olive oil in a large ovenproof skillet over medium-high heat. Add the chicken pieces and garlic cloves and brown well.

3. Turn the chicken pieces, skin side down, and pour the lemon juice and stock into the pan. Sprinkle with salt and pepper and bake for 20 minutes. Remove the pan from the oven, and turn the pieces, skin side up. Bake for 15 minutes more for breasts and 20 minutes more for dark meat. Remove the pan from the oven.

4. Place the chicken pieces on a serving platter, and scatter the garlic cloves around them. Bring the sauce back to a boil on the stove and reduce by one fourth. Add a few teaspoons of the cornstarch mixture at a time until the sauce is just lightly thickened. Serve immediately.

*Note:* The dish can be prepared up to 1 day in advance and reheated in a 300°F. oven until hot, about 15 minutes.

# Smoked Turkey Salad

[ Serves 6 ]

**Smoked Turkey Salad**

1 1/2 pounds smoked turkey, cut into
    1/2-inch dice

4 hard-boiled eggs, peeled and diced

1 cup cooked corn kernels

One 15-ounce can red kidney beans,
    drained and rinsed

1 small red onion, peeled and minced

2 celery stalks, trimmed and thinly sliced

**Dressing**

1/2 cup My Favorite Barbecue Sauce (page 173)

2 garlic cloves, minced

2 tablespoons chopped cilantro

1/3 cup mayonnaise

Aromatic and tender smoked turkey is the centerpiece of this appetizing salad. The key to its lively flavor is the homemade barbecue sauce. It's easy to smoke turkeys yourself in a covered grill, and the flavor is superior to any purchased cold cut.

*The large celery stalks around the outside of a head can be tough and fibrous. Starting at the tip, break off the top inch and it will be attached to the strings, which can then be easily pulled off.*

1. To prepare the salad, combine the turkey, eggs, corn, beans, onion, and celery in a mixing bowl.
2. To prepare the dressing, whisk together the barbecue sauce, garlic, cilantro, and mayonnaise. Toss the dressing with the salad ingredients and serve chilled.

*Note:* The salad can be prepared 1 day in advance and refrigerated, tightly covered.

When I first started cooking more than thirty years ago, the only time you'd find turkeys in the market was the week before Thanksgiving. I now use lean turkey breast in many ways, such as this quickly-prepared stew, which is a variation on Italian veal marsala. Serve it with orzo or egg noodles and a steamed green vegetable.

*This is a good dish to serve at a buffet dinner. You can vary it by using fresh shiitake mushrooms and adding some halved baby carrots.*

# Turkey Stew with Marsala and Sage
[ Serves 6 ]

4 tablespoons olive oil

2 pounds turkey breast meat, cut into 1-inch cubes

2 tablespoons unsalted butter

1/2 pound mushrooms, rinsed, trimmed and halved if large

2 medium onions, peeled and diced

3 garlic cloves, minced

2 cups turkey stock or Chicken Stock (page 63)

1/2 dry marsala wine

2 tablespoons chopped fresh sage or 1 teaspoon dried sage

Salt and freshly ground black pepper to taste

1 tablespoon cornstarch mixed with 2 tablespoons cold water

*1.* Heat 2 tablespoons of the olive oil in a large skillet over medium-high heat. Add the turkey, and brown on all sides. Remove the turkey from the pan with a slotted spoon and set aside. Add the remaining olive oil and butter to the pan, and heat over medium heat. Add the mushrooms, onions, and garlic. Sauté, stirring frequently, for 3 to 5 minutes, or until the onions are translucent.

*2.* Add the stock, marsala, sage, and salt and pepper to the pan. Bring to a boil over high heat and boil until reduced by half, stirring frequently. Return the turkey to the pan and cook over low heat, uncovered, for 20 minutes, stirring occasionally.

*3.* Stir the cornstarch mixture into the stew and cook over low heat for 2 minutes, or until the mixture is lightly thickened.

*Note:* The stew can be made up to 2 days in advance and refrigerated, tightly covered. Reheat it, covered, over low heat, stirring occasionally.

# Braised Short Ribs of Beef

[ Serve 6 ]

7 pounds meaty short ribs

Salt and freshly ground black pepper

1/2 cup all-purpose flour

3 tablespoons vegetable oil

1 cup diced onion

1 cup diced celery

4 garlic cloves, minced

1 1/2 cups beef stock

2 tablespoons chopped fresh rosemary
or 2 teaspoons dried rosemary

*1.* Preheat the oven to 350°F.

*2.* Season the ribs with salt and pepper and dust them with flour, shaking off the excess. Heat the oil in a large Dutch oven or ovenproof casserole over medium-high heat. Add the ribs, being careful to not crowd the pan, and brown on all sides.

*3.* Remove the ribs from the pan with tongs and set aside. Add the onion, celery, and garlic to the pan and sauté over medium heat for 5 minutes, stirring constantly. Return the ribs to the pan and add the stock and rosemary. Bring to a boil, cover the pan, and bake for 2 to 2 1/2 hours, or until the meat is fork-tender, turning the ribs occasionally with tongs.  Remove the pan from the oven and tilt the pan. Spoon off and discard as much of the grease as possible.

*Note:* The dish can be prepared up to 2 days in advance and refrigerated, tightly covered. Remove and discard the layer of solid fat from the top. Reheat the ribs, covered, in a 350°F. oven for 25 minutes, or until hot.

The aroma that fills the house when meats are braising is a winter treat. An excellent cut of beef for slow-cooked dishes is short ribs; they become meltingly tender. Serve them over buttered egg noodles or wild rice with a tossed salad.

*The poet Saki wrote that "beef is the soul of cooking."*

*If you can't find short ribs of beef, cut a chuck roast into two-inch cubes for this recipe.*

Entrée salads that combine hot grilled food with crisp cold greens have been gaining in popularity during the past decade. This salad's Asian marinade/dressing contrasts sweet hoisin sauce and mellow rice wine vinegar to achieve complex flavor.

# Asian Steak Salad

[ Serves  6 ]

Dressing

1/3 cup rice wine vinegar

3 tablespoons soy sauce

3 tablespoons Dijon mustard

2 tablespoons hoisin sauce

3 tablespoons grated fresh ginger

4 garlic cloves, minced

2 scallions, trimmed and finely chopped

Freshly ground black pepper to taste

3/4 cup vegetable oil

1/4 cup Asian sesame oil

Salad

One 2-pound flank steak

1/4 pound snow peas, tips removed

1 pound baby spinach leaves, rinsed and stemmed

1/4 pound bean sprouts, rinsed

2 cucumbers, peeled, halved, and thinly sliced

1 red bell pepper, seeds and ribs removed, thinly sliced

1. To prepare the dressing, combine the vinegar, soy sauce, mustard, hoisin sauce, ginger, garlic, scallions, and pepper in a jar with a tight-fitting lid. Shake well. Add the vegetable and sesame oils and shake well again.

2. To prepare the steak, score the flank steak in a diagonal pattern 1/4 inch deep. Place the steak in a heavy plastic bag and add 1/2 cup of the dressing. Marinate, refrigerated, for 4 hours, turning the bag occasionally so that the steak marinates evenly.

3. Light a charcoal or gas grill. Place the snow peas in a microwave-safe container with 1 tablespoon of water. Microwave on HIGH (100%) for 30 seconds. Plunge the snow peas into a bowl of ice water. Drain. Combine the snow peas with the spinach, bean sprouts, cucumbers, and red pepper in a salad bowl.

4. Grill the steak to desired doneness. Allow the meat to rest for 5 minutes, then thinly slice it on the diagonal.

5. To serve, toss the salad with 1/3 cup of the vinaigrette. Divide it among the plates, top the greens with steak slices, and pass the remaining dressing separately.

*Note:* This dish can also be made with leftover grilled steak. Drizzle the meat with 1/3 cup of the vinaigrette before serving.

*You can substitute slices of grilled chicken breast or fish steaks for the beef in this recipe. If served as an appetizer, the recipe will feed eight to ten people.*

A creamy chili sauce dotted with fresh corn kernels turns a basic grilled steak to a fancy party dish. The same sauce can be used with equal success on chicken and seafood.

76

# Grilled Steak with Southwest Corn Sauce
[ Serves 6 ]

Grilled Steak

Six 8-ounce ribeye or sirloin strip steaks

1 tablespoon herbes de provence

1 tablespoon dry mustard

4 garlic cloves, minced

Salt and freshly ground black pepper to taste

Southwest Corn Sauce

4 ears fresh corn, shucked

2 tablespoons olive oil

1 small onion, peeled and diced

1 red bell pepper, seeds and ribs removed, finely chopped

3 tablespoons chili powder

1/2 cup dry red wine

3 cups beef stock

1/2 cup heavy cream

*1.* To prepare the steak, trim the steaks of excess fat. Combine the herbes de provence, mustard, garlic, and salt and pepper in a small bowl. Rub the mixture on both sides of the steaks and refrigerate the meat, tightly covered with plastic wrap for 30 minutes.

*2.* Light a charcoal or gas grill.

*3.* To prepare the corn sauce, cut the kernels from the corn using a sharp serrated knife. Place one fourth of the kernels in a food processor fitted with a steel blade or in a blender and puree until smooth. Heat the oil in a saucepan over low heat. Add the onion and red pepper and sauté, stirring frequently, for 3 minutes. Add the chili powder and stir over low heat for 2 minutes. Add the wine, stock, and pureed corn to the pan and boil over medium heat, stirring occasionally, until the mixture is reduced by half. Add the cream and corn kernels to the sauce and cook over medium heat for 5 minutes, stirring occasionally. Season with salt and pepper and keep the sauce hot.

*4.* Grill the steaks to desired doneness. Top the steaks with some of the sauce, and serve immediately

*Note:* The sauce can be prepared up to 2 days in advance and refrigerated, tightly covered. Reheat it over low heat, stirring occasionally.

*Maize, the grain we know as corn, has been raised in North America for more than two thousand years. It served as the staple of the Native American diet, and most tribes had deities that were responsible for raising successful corn crops. It was the Native Americans who added popcorn to our repertoire of snack foods.*

*Always turn foods that are grilling or broiling with tongs rather than a fork. A fork will pierce the seared surface and allow juices to escape.*

Two foods in the foundation of New England cookery are tart cranberries and sweet maple syrup. The herbed cranberry marinade creates tender and succulent ribs that become golden brown when glazed with maple as they grill.

*I've also used this marinade for grilled chicken and pork chops.*

*Early New England settlers sweetened foods with maple syrup because white sugar was expensive since it had to be imported. While there were maple trees in Europe, the sugar maples found in North America are native to this continent. How to tap the trees and create syrup from the sap is another skill taught by the Native Americans.*

# Cranberry-Maple Spareribs

[ Serves 6 ]

1 cup cranberry juice

2 tablespoons orange juice concentrate

4 garlic cloves, minced

1 shallot, minced

1 tablespoon fresh thyme or 1 teaspoon dried thyme

1/2 teaspoon ground allspice

Salt and freshly ground black pepper to taste

4 pounds baby back ribs, cut into 6 servings

1/3 cup maple syrup

1. Combine the cranberry juice, orange juice concentrate, garlic, shallot, thyme, allspice, and salt and pepper in a large heavy plastic bag. Mix well and add the ribs. Marinate the ribs, refrigerated, for 12 to 18 hours, turning the bag occasionally so the ribs marinate evenly.

2. Light a charcoal or gas grill. Remove the ribs from the marinade and reserve the marinade. Grill the ribs, turning them occasionally, until almost cooked through, about 20 minutes. While the ribs are grilling, combine the reserved marinade and maple syrup in a small saucepan and boil over medium heat until reduced to 1/3 cup. Brush the underside of the ribs with the glaze and grill for 2 minutes. Turn the ribs, brush the top side, and grill for 2 minutes more.

*Note:* The ribs can be grilled 1 day in advance. Reheat them in a 375°F. oven and brush them with additional glaze.

# Grilled Caribbean Pork Chops

[ Serves 6 ]

Six 1-inch-thick pork chops

1 large onion, peeled and chopped

4 garlic cloves, minced

1 tablespoon dried thyme

1 tablespoon sugar

1 1/2 teaspoons cayenne

1 teaspoon freshly ground black pepper

1 teaspoon ground allspice

1/2 teaspoon ground cinnamon

Salt to taste

---

1. Prepare a charcoal or gas grill.
2. Trim the excess fat from the pork chops and set the chops aside. Combine the onion, garlic, thyme, sugar, cayenne, black pepper, allspice, cinnamon, and salt in a blender and puree.
3. Rub the pork chops on both sides with the spice paste and grill over hot coals for 5 to 6 minutes on each side, or until cooked through.

*Note:* Instead of pork chops, use the same rub on a 2-pound pork loin. Bake it in a 375°F. oven for 45 minutes, or until a meat thermometer reads 145°F.

Aromatic allspice and cinnamon are characteristic flavors of Caribbean cooking. One of the advantages of the paste rub that flavors these chops is that no time is needed for marinating. I serve these chops with rice and stewed black beans.

*True cinnamon is the bark from a tropical tree grown in Asia, but most of what we call cinnamon is actually a related bark from the cassia tree.*

*Allspice, one of the characteristic flavors of ketchup, is so named because its aroma is reminiscent of a blend of cloves, cinnamon, and nutmeg. The taste, however, is pungent, like pepper. Its original name was Jamaica pepper.*

This hearty dish is emblematic of fall, when the weather is still warm enough to light the grill and the yearly apple harvest has begun. The sweet apples pair well with the flavorful, tender pork. Serve this dish with Braised Red Cabbage (page 148) and some mashed potatoes.

*There are more than three hundred varieties of apples grown in North America, although none of them were native to the continent. The first apple seeds were brought from England by the Pilgrims in 1620. Granny Smith are a relative newcomer to the apple world, and one reason they're gaining popularity is that they hold their shape while being cooked. They were brought over in the mid-19th century from Australia.*

# Smoky Pork Chops with Apples

[ Serves 6 ]

2 pounds boneless pork loin, cut into 6 slices

1/4 cup maple syrup

2 tablespoons kosher salt

1 cup water

1 cup hickory chips

2 tablespoons unsalted butter

1/2 cup maple syrup

1 tablespoon cinnamon

3 cooking apples, such as Granny Smith, cored and cut into 12 slices each

1. Place the pork in a 1-gallon plastic bag. Add the maple syrup, salt, and water. Marinate the pork, refrigerated, for 24 hours.

2. Light a charcoal or gas grill. Soak the hickory chips in water for 30 minutes.

3. Remove the pork from the marinade and discard the marinade. Drain the hickory chips and place them on the grill. Cook the pork for 6 to 8 minutes on each side, or until just slightly pink in the center.

4. While the pork is cooking, heat the butter in a large skillet over medium heat. Combine the maple syrup and cinnamon. Add the apples to the pan, and baste the slices with the maple mixture. Cook the apples over medium heat, turning them gently with tongs, for 6 minutes, or until cooked but still retaining texture. Remove the pan from the heat and keep the apples warm.

5. To serve, top each pork chop with some of the apple slices.

*Note:* The apples can be prepared 1 day in advance and refrigerated, tightly covered. Reheat them over low heat, stirring gently occasionally.

## Stuffed Grilled Veal Chops

[ Serves 6 ]

Six 1-inch-thick veal chops

Salt and freshly ground black pepper to taste

6 thick slices of prosciutto, cut into strips

1/4 pound fontina cheese

2 sprigs of fresh sage or 2 teaspoons dried sage

1 1/2 cups of your favorite tomato sauce or spaghetti sauce, heated (optional)

1. Light a charcoal or gas grill.
2. Cut a horizontal pocket into each of the veal chops, and sprinkle the chops with salt and pepper. Place the prosciutto, cheese, and sage in a food processor fitted with a steel blade and chop fine. Stuff the veal chops with the mixture. Secure the chops closed with toothpicks.
3. Grill the chops for 4 to 6 minutes on each side, or until cooked to desired doneness. Serve immediately, topped with tomato sauce, if desired.

*Note:* The chops can be stuffed up to 3 hours in advance and refrigerated, tightly covered. They can also be cooked in a preheated oven broiler.

*Part of the elegance of Italian cooking is its simplicity, and this veal dish embodies that principle. The herbed cheese and prosciutto stuffing moistens and flavors the tender veal, and a sauce is not really necessary. I serve these chops with pasta and a tossed salad.*

*You can use the same stuffing for pork chops or chicken breasts that have not been boned.*

*More veal is consumed per capita in Italy than in any other country. Noted food authority Waverley Root wrote that this is because the Italians are such excellent sauce makers, and the delicacy of veal allows the sauces to dominate a dish.*

This is an elegant dinner entree that appears complex and belies how easy it is to make. The veal scallops are baked until tender with woodsy wild mushrooms and luscious cheese. It's a good dish to make for a large crowd, since it does not require any per portion attention.

# Baked Veal Gratin with Wild Mushrooms

[ Serves 6 ]

1 1/2 pounds veal scallops

Salt and freshly ground black pepper to taste

4 tablespoons (1/2 stick) unsalted butter

4 cups diced onions

1/2 pound fresh shiitake mushrooms, stemmed and sliced

1 1/2 cups plain breadcrumbs

2 cups grated Gruyère cheese

1 1/4 cups Chicken Stock (page 63) or veal stock

1 1/4 cups dry white wine

*1.* Preheat the oven to 350°F.

*2.* Pound the veal scallops between 2 sheets of wax paper or plastic wrap to an even thickness of 1/4 inch. Season them with salt and pepper and set aside.

*3.* Melt 2 tablespoons of the butter in a sauté pan over medium heat. Add the onions and stir to coat them well. Cover the pan and cook the onions over low heat for 10 minutes, stirring occasionally. Uncover the pan, raise the heat to medium-high, and sprinkle the onions lightly with salt. Sauté until limp but not brown, about 5 minutes, stirring frequently.

*4.* Scrape the onions into a 9 X 13-inch gratin pan or baking dish. Add the remaining butter to the pan and melt it over medium-high heat. Add the sliced mushrooms, sprinkle lightly with salt and pepper, and sauté until they are soft and brown, about 5 minutes. Set aside.

*5.* Mix the breadcrumbs with 1 1/2 cups of the grated cheese and press this mixture into the veal scallops. Place overlapping veal slices on top of the onions, and scatter the sautéed mushrooms over them. Sprinkle the remaining cheese on top, and pour the stock and water over the dish.

*6.* Bake for 1 hour 15 minutes, checking after 45 minutes and adding more stock or wine if the dish seems to be dry. Serve immediately.

*Note:* The dish can be assembled for baking up to adding the stock and wine 1 day in advance and refrigerated, tightly covered with plastic wrap. Add 10 minutes to the baking time.

83

For good veal, the animal is fed on its mother's milk rather than grain to ensure tender, pink meat. Most milk-fed veal comes from three- to four-month-old calves; older animals have usually started to eat grass and are on their way to becoming young cows. The meat of grass-fed veal is darker and coarser, with neither the full-flavored richness of beef nor the delicacy of milk-fed veal.

While rosemary and garlic are a traditional rub for rosy, tender lamb, I find the addition of lemon zest balances the meat's natural richness. While this dish can be prepared entirely on the grill, or entirely in the oven, this dual cooking method relieves the need for split-second timing.

*Lamb plays an important role in Nantucket's history. The earliest European settlers had common land on which sheep grazed. Ram Pasture, now part of the island's conservation land near Miacomet Pond, was so named since the shepherds would herd rams across a narrow bridge to keep them away from the ewes at certain times of year. In the 17th century the island's largest celebration was Sheep Shearing Day in June; the wool was as prized a cash crop as whale oil.*

84

# Grilled Leg of Lamb with Garlic, Rosemary, and Lemon
[ Serves 6 ]

1/2 leg of lamb, boned, rolled, and tied, to yield 3 pounds meat

10 garlic cloves, peeled

Zest of 1 lemon, cut into thin strips

3 sprigs of rosemary, leaves removed

1 tablespoon kosher salt

1 teaspoon freshly ground black pepper

1/2 cup beef stock

1. Allow the meat to reach room temperature and cut deep slits into any thick portions with a paring knife.

2. Light a charcoal or gas grill.

3. Combine the garlic, lemon zest, and rosemary leaves in a food processor fitted with a steel blade and chop finely using an on and off pulsing action. Scrape the mixture into a small bowl and stir in the salt and pepper. Stuff the garlic mixture into all the crevices of the meat formed when it was boned, as well as into the slits. Rub some of the mixture all over the surface of the roast.

4. Preheat the oven to 350°F.

5. When the coals are just beginning to cover over with gray ash and the fire is very hot, sear the roast, turning it gently with tongs, for 7 to 10 minutes, or until the exterior is browned on all sides. Remove it from the grill and place it in a roasting pan.

6. Roast the lamb, uncovered, for 45 to 60 minutes, or until the temperature registers 125°F. on a meat thermometer; the roasting time will depend on the thickness of the roll. Remove the lamb from the oven and place it on a platter lightly covered with aluminum foil for 15 minutes to allow the juices to be reabsorbed into the meat.

7. Pour the grease out of the roasting pan and pour in the stock. Place the pan back into the oven and bake, stirring from time to time to dislodge any brown bits clinging to the bottom of the pan. Carve the meat into slices, adding any juices to the pan, and pass the sauce separately.

*Note:* If cooking the roast entirely in the oven, roast it for 15 minutes at 500°F., then reduce the oven temperature to 350°F., and follow the procedure outlined above.

# Braised Lamb Shanks

[ Serves 6 ]

6 lamb shanks

1/2 cup all-purpose flour

Salt and freshly ground black pepper to taste

1/2 teaspoon dried oregano

1/3 cup olive oil

3/4 cup chopped onions

3/4 cup chopped celery

3/4 cup chopped carrots

3 tablespoons coarsely minced garlic

2 teaspoons fresh thyme or 1/2 teaspoon dried thyme

1 tablespoon chopped fresh rosemary or 1 teaspoon dried rosemary

2 tablespoons tomato paste

1 cup Barolo, or other dry red wine

3/4 cup beef stock

1. Preheat the oven to 350°F.

2. Wipe the lamb shanks well with a damp cloth and remove any fat. Combine the flour, salt and pepper, and oregano and dredge the lamb shanks in the seasoned flour, shaking off any excess. Heat the oil in a skillet over medium-high heat and brown the lamb shanks on all sides, turning them with tongs. Transfer the shanks to a Dutch oven as they are browned. Add the onions, celery, carrots, garlic, thyme, and rosemary to the skillet and cook, stirring, for 5 minutes.

3. Add the vegetables to the lamb along with the tomato paste, wine, and stock. Bring to a boil on top of the stove, then cover and bake for 1 1/2 to 2 hours, or until meat is tender.

4. Remove the shanks to a warm platter and tip the casserole to be able to spoon off as much grease as possible. Cook the sauce over medium heat until reduced by half, then pour it over the shanks.

*Note:* The shanks can be prepared up to 3 days in advance and refrigerated. If cooked in advance, remove the layer of grease, which will have hardened on the top. Reheat, covered, in a 350°F. oven for 25 to 35 minutes, or until hot.

*I'm truly a peasant at heart, and I adore slow-cooked braised dishes made from less expensive cuts of meat. When cooking lamb shanks I always think of the sensuous eating scene from the movie* Tom Jones, *since the shanks are so large. Serve the shanks with buttered noodles or polenta.*

*An old Spanish trick for tenderizing meats that have to braise slowly, such as shanks or briskets, is to add a few wine corks to the pan. Cork releases an enzyme that penetrates the meats to tenderize them. Just remember to remove the corks before serving.*

85

Shepherd's Pie is part of the English tradition that Nantucket's first European settlers brought to the island, and it's still served in British pubs today. This is a wonderful dish for a fall or winter buffet, since all it needs is a green salad to complete the meal.

# Shepherd's Pie

[ Serves  6 to 8 ]

### Lamb Filling

2 pounds lean ground lamb

4 tablespoons unsalted butter

3 tablespoons olive oil

1/2 pound fresh shiitake mushrooms, stemmed and sliced

2 onions, peeled and diced

6 garlic cloves, minced

2 cups dry red wine

1 package Knorr's mushroom gravy mix

2 tablespoons chopped fresh rosemary leaves or 2 teaspoons dried rosemary

1 tablespoon chopped fresh thyme or 1 teaspoon dried thyme

One 1-pound package frozen mixed vegetables

### Potato Topping

2 pounds redskin potatoes, scrubbed and cut into 1-inch dice

1/2 cup heavy cream

4 tablespoons unsalted butter

2 cups grated sharp Cheddar cheese

Salt and freshly ground black pepper to taste

1. To prepare the filling, place a large skillet over medium-high heat. Add the lamb, breaking it up with a fork, and brown it well. Remove the lamb from the skillet and set aside. Heat 2 tablespoons of the butter and 1 tablespoon of the oil in the skillet over medium-high heat. Add the mushrooms and sauté, stirring constantly, for 3 minutes, or until the mushrooms are soft. Scrape the mushrooms into the bowl with the lamb.

2. Heat the remaining butter and oil in the skillet over medium heat. Add the onions and garlic and sauté, stirring constantly, for 3 minutes, or until the onions are translucent. Return the lamb and mushrooms to the skillet and add the wine, gravy mix, rosemary, and thyme. Bring to a boil, reduce the heat to low, and simmer the mixture, uncovered, for 30 minutes, or until thickened. Tilt the pan to spoon off as much grease as possible.

3. Prepare the topping while the lamb is simmering. Place the potatoes in a saucepan, cover them with salted water, and bring to a boil over high heat. Reduce the heat to medium and boil the potatoes, uncovered, for 12 to 15 minutes, or until soft. Drain the potatoes. Heat the cream, butter, and Cheddar cheese in the saucepan over medium heat until the cheese is melted, stirring occasionally. Return the potatoes to the saucepan and mash well with a potato masher. Set aside.

4. Preheat the oven to 425°F.

5. Add the mixed vegetables to the lamb and bring the mixture back to a boil. Simmer for 3 minutes, then scrape the mixture into a 9 X 13-inch baking dish. Spoon the potatoes on top of the lamb, smoothing them into an even layer. Bake for 15 minutes, or until the lamb is bubbly and the potatoes are lightly browned. Serve immediately.

*Note:* The lamb mixture can be prepared 2 days in advance and refrigerated, tightly covered. Reheat it over low heat or in a microwave oven before placing it in the baking dish. The potatoes can be prepared 3 hours in advance and kept at room temperature.

*When baking a casserole such as this one, always place it on a foil-covered baking sheet. It's inevitable that some juices will bubble over the side, and the baking sheet saves cleaning the oven later.*

# Two if by Sea:
## Fish & Seafood Entrees

This salad epitomizes Nantucket in late summer, when fresh corn is in season. The sweetness of the corn is a perfect foil to the lobster, and the remaining ingredients glorify these two stars.

*My friend Ann Brody Cove taught me the perfect way to cook corn. Bring a large pot of salted water to a boil, and add a few tablespoons of sugar. Add the corn, cover the pot, and as soon as the water returns to a boil, turn off the heat. Let the pot sit without removing the cover for 5 minutes, and your corn will be perfect. The beauty of this method is that the corn stops cooking and stays hot, so you can leave it in the water and serve it an hour later.*

# Lobster and Corn Salad
[ Serves 6 ]

1 1/2 pounds cooked lobster meat

6 ears of corn, cooked and chilled

1/2 cup mayonnaise

1/3 cup cocktail sauce

1 cup finely diced celery

1/3 cup finely diced red onion

3 tablespoons chopped dill

Salt and freshly ground black pepper to taste

6 leaves Boston lettuce

90

1. Cut the lobster meat into 1/2-inch dice, and set aside. Cut the kernels off the corn and combine them with the lobster in a mixing bowl. Add the mayonnaise, cocktail sauce, celery, red onion, and dill. Stir gently to combine. Season with salt and pepper.
2. To serve, mound the salad into the lettuce leaves.

*Note:* The salad can be made 1 day in advance and refrigerated, tightly covered.

# Thai Lobster Salad

[ Serves 6 to 8 ]

## Dressing

1/3 cup freshly squeezed lime juice

1/4 cup Thai or Vietnamese fish sauce

1/4 cup vegetable oil

2 tablespoons sugar

2 slices fresh ginger, about the size of
   a quarter, 1/4 inch thick

2 to 3 jalapeño chilies, stemmed
   and seeded

3 cloves garlic, peeled

3/4 cup (firmly packed) basil leaves

## Lobster Salad

1 1/2 pounds lobster meat

8 ounces thin rice noodles, cooked according
   to package directions and chilled

1 English cucumber, trimmed, halved
   and thinly sliced

1 small red onion, peeled and thinly sliced

10 ounces spinach, stemmed, rinsed,
   and shredded

1. To prepare the dressing, combine all the dressing ingredients in a food processor fitted with a steel blade and puree. Refrigerate.

2. To prepare the salad, cut the lobster meat into 1-inch cubes and combine it with the cooked rice noodles, cucumber, and red onion in a mixing bowl. Add the dressing and mix well. To serve, mound the shredded spinach on a platter and mound the salad in the center.

*Note:* The lobster can be cooked and the dressing can be prepared 1 day in advance and refrigerated, tightly covered. Do not dress the salad more than 2 hours before serving.

This salad is similar to one I recall eating in Thailand a few years ago. It's slightly spicy, but the chilies are balanced by the refreshing fresh basil. Since delicate cellophane noodles are part of the dish, they stretch the lobster meat to feed a larger crowd.

*To give the lobster salad a stunning presentation as part of a buffet, use a huge lobster rather than a few small ones. Remove the tail meat by cutting the tail on the underside, and carefully remove the top shell, saving the body for stock. Cut an opening in the body shell, and mound the salad inside it. Mound additional salad in the overturned tail shell.*

Grilling adds a slightly smoky nuance to the succulent lobster meat, and the flavor of the garlic and herbs in the butter seeps into the lobster as well as keeping the meat moist as it grills. Some simple sliced tomatoes and potato salad make this a summertime feast.

*While there is no difference in the flavor of a male or female lobster, the bright red roe from the females adds a rosy color to stocks and can be sprinkled over salads as a garnish. To determine the female lobster, compare two lobsters of similar size. The one with the broader abdomen and tail is the female. The female also has smaller, more flexible swimmerets, which are the first pair of legs at the base of the tail.*

# Grilled Lobster with Herb Butter Sauce

[ Serves 6 ]

Six 1 1/2-pound live lobsters

1/2 cup (1 stick) unsalted butter

4 garlic cloves, minced

2 tablespoons freshly squeezed lemon juice

2 tablespoons chopped parsley

2 teaspoons herbes de provence

1 teaspoon grated lemon zest

Salt and freshly ground black pepper to taste

*1.* Bring a lobster pot of salted water to a boil. Add the lobsters, head first, and cover the pot. When the water returns to a boil, cook the lobsters for 5 minutes. Remove the lobsters from the water with tongs, and run cold tap water over the lobsters to cool them.

*2.* Heat a charcoal or gas grill.

*3.* Place a lobster on a large cutting board with the top of its shell up. Cut the lobster in half lengthwise. Remove and discard the black vein running down the lobster tail, and the sand sac located at the top of the head. Repeat with the remaining lobsters.

*4.* Melt the butter in a small saucepan over low heat. Add the garlic, lemon juice, parsley, herbes de provence, lemon zest, and salt and pepper. Stir well. Place the lobsters on the grill rack, cut side up. Cover the grill and cook for 2 minutes. Drizzle the lobsters with half the butter, cover the grill, and cook for 3 minutes more, or until the meat in the tail is firm. Remove the lobsters from the grill and drizzle with the remaining butter. Serve immediately.

*Note:* The lobsters can be prepared for grilling a few hours in advance.

# Spicy Southwest Shrimp

[ Serves 6 ]

2 pounds large raw shrimp, peeled and deveined

1/4 pound bacon, finely sliced

2 medium onions, peeled and diced

5 garlic cloves, minced

3 jalapeño peppers, seeds and ribs removed, finely chopped

1 tablespoon ground cumin

2 medium tomatoes, cored, seeded, and diced

One 15-ounce can pinto beans, drained and rinsed

1 cup Lobster Stock (page 62) or bottled clam juice

1/4 cup olive oil

2 tablespoons chopped cilantro

2 teaspoons fresh thyme or 1/2 teaspoon dried thyme

Salt and freshly ground black pepper to taste

Freshly squeezed lime juice to taste

*1.* Rinse the shrimp and set aside. Place the bacon in a saucepan over medium-high heat. Cook the bacon until almost crisp, then add the onion and garlic to the pan. Lower the heat to medium, and cook for 2 minutes, stirring constantly. Add the jalapeño and cumin and continue to cook for 1 minute. Add the tomato, beans, and stock to the pan. Bring to a boil, reduce the heat to low, and simmer for 10 minutes.

*2.* When the sauce has almost completed simmering, place a sauté pan over high heat and heat the oil until hot. Add the shrimp and sear on both sides. Add the bean mixture to the pan, along with the cilantro and thyme. Lower the heat to medium and cook for about 2 minutes, or until the shrimp are cooked through. Season with salt and pepper and lime juice to taste. Serve immediately.

*Note:* The bean mixture can be prepared 1 day in advance and refrigerated, tightly covered. Reheat it over low heat in a saucepan. Cook the shrimp just before serving.

While shrimp are not native to the cold waters of the North Atlantic, they are one of the most popular dishes served on Nantucket as well as the rest of the nation. This spicy preparation is easy to make and elegant. Serve it on slices of toasted corn bread with a tossed salad.

*When cutting chili peppers, rub the hand holding the pepper with vegetable oil to avoid getting the potent chili oil on your skin. Then carve down the sides of the pepper and remove the flesh. The seeds will remain attached to the ribs, and then you can discard the whole unit.*

Admittedly, this recipe is more complex and more work than boiling a lobster in a pot, but the result is well worth the trouble. It's beautiful; the bright green creamed spinach is a visual contrast to the bright red lobster. And the ginger and Sauternes *beurre blanc* accentuates the sweetness of this prized crustacean.

# Lobster with Ginger, Lime, and Sauternes

[ Serves 6 ]

Six 1 1/2-pound live lobsters

1/4 cup finely chopped fresh ginger

1 cup Sauternes or other sweet
    late-harvest white wine

3/4 pound (3 sticks) unsalted butter,
    cut into 1-tablespoon pieces, cold

1 1/2 pounds spinach, rinsed and stemmed

2 limes, zest grated and juiced

Salt and freshly ground pepper to taste

1/4 cup heavy cream

Garnish

2 tablespoons finely chopped candied ginger

1/2 cup finely diced mango

1/4 cup finely diced avocado

1/4 cup finely diced red bell pepper

2 tablespoons minced chives

94

1. Bring a large lobster pot of salted water to a boil over high heat. When rapidly boiling, plunge the lobsters into the pot, head first. When the water returns to a boil, boil for 10 minutes, and drain. When cool enough to handle, break off the claws and arms and remove the meat. Cut the body and tail in half lengthwise, and cut the tail meat into 6 pieces. Remove the meat from the tail and rinse out the shell to remove the tomalley. Set the meat and shells aside.

2. Place the ginger and Sauternes in a small saucepan. Bring to a boil, reduce the heat, and simmer until all the liquid that remains is 2 tablespoons of a thick syrup. Set aside.

3. Heat 2 tablespoons of the butter in a large sauté pan or skillet over medium-high heat. Add the spinach and stir until the spinach wilts and turns bright green, about 1 minute. Remove the spinach from the pan and drain well in a colander, pressing out the liquid with the back of a spoon. Set aside.

4. To finish the dish, heat the ginger and Sauternes reduction over low heat. Add the remaining butter, a few tablespoons at a time, swirling each time until the butter is incorporated before adding the next piece of butter. The sauce cannot come to a boil, but if it gets too cool to incorporate the butter, place it back over low heat for a few seconds. Add all the remaining butter, then stir in the lime zest, salt and pepper, and enough lime juice to create a sweet/sour balance.

5. To serve, stir the cream into the spinach and season with salt and pepper. Warm the spinach. Divide the spinach among the body cavities of the lobsters. If necessary, reheat the lobster meat in a 350°F. oven for 5 minutes, covered. Remove the meat, squeeze to extract any water, place the claw meat over the spinach, and arrange the tail meat in the tail. Spoon the sauce over the meat and sprinkle with the candied ginger, mango, avocado, red pepper, and chives.

*Note:* The lobster can be cooked 1 day in advance and refrigerated, tightly covered. The sauce can be made up to 2 hours in advance and poured into a heated thermos bottle.

95

*If possible, ask the fishmonger for some of the seaweed in which the lobster was transported. Rinse it and add it to the cooking pot; the water will taste more like sea water.*

*If you are buying lobsters early in the day they're going to be cooked, store them refrigerated, wrapped in a few layers of wet newspaper or paper towels. It will keep them fresher.*

Alas, our beloved Nantucket bay scallops are only fished from November to March, so during summer grilling season I turn to larger sea scallops for this Caribbean-inspired dish. The salsa and slightly spicy dressing enliven the grilled mollusks.

# Grilled Scallops with Mango and Chili Vinaigrette

[ Serves 6 ]

2 pounds sea scallops

Mango Salsa

1 large, ripe mango, peeled, seeded, and cut into a 1/4-inch dice

1/2 cup diced (1/4 inch) English cucumber

1/2 cup finely chopped red onion

1/4 cup roasted and diced red bell pepper

3 tablespoons chopped cilantro

1 tablespoon olive oil

2 tablespoons freshly squeezed lime juice

Salt and freshly ground black pepper to taste

Chili Vinaigrette

1/2 cup roasted and diced red bell pepper

1/3 cup cider vinegar

2/3 cup olive oil

1/4 to 3/4 teaspoon Chinese chili oil, to taste

Salt and freshly ground black pepper to taste

*1.* Thread the scallops horizontally onto bamboo skewers, and refrigerate until ready to grill.

*2.* To prepare the salsa, combine the salsa ingredients in a glass or stainless steel mixing bowl. Stir gently and allow to sit at room temperature for at least 30 minutes to blend the flavors.

*3.* To prepare the vinaigrette, combine the red pepper and vinegar in a food processor fitted with a steel blade or in a blender. With the motor running, slowly add the olive oil and chili oil through the feed tube to emulsify the dressing. Season with salt and pepper and set aside.

*4.* Light a charcoal or gas grill. Season the scallops with salt and pepper, brush them with the vinaigrette, and grill the skewers for 1 1/2 to 2 minutes on each side.

*5.* To serve, drizzle some of the vinaigrette over the skewers and place the salsa next to them on the plate.

*Note:* The dressing and salsa can be made 1 day in advance and refrigerated. Allow the salsa to reach room temperature before grilling the scallops.

*This recipe will serve eight to ten as an appetizer.*

*If the mango is hard to peel, try to peel it from the other end. Every mango has an easy and hard way to peel it.*

97

Robert Kinkead, now a culinary legend in Washington, DC, was still chef at 21 Federal here when I started visiting Nantucket more than a decade ago. He served a seafood stew similar to this one, which included garlicky Portuguese sausage as well as a myriad of aquatic species. It's one of my favorite winter dishes. If you can't find linguiça, any garlicky, spicy sausage can be substituted.

## Nantucket Seafood Stew with Red Pepper Rouille

[ Serves 6 to 8 ]

**Seafood Stew**

1/4 pound bacon, diced

1 medium onion, peeled and diced

1 carrot, peeled and diced

1 celery stalk, diced

3 garlic cloves, minced

1 pound mild linguiça sausage, diced

3 large tomatoes, peeled, seeded, and chopped

2 oranges, zest grated and juiced

1/2 cup white wine

3 cups fish stock or clam juice

2 tablespoons chopped parsley

2 teaspoons fresh thyme or 1/2 teaspoon dried thyme

1 bay leaf

3 tablespoons chopped fresh basil or 1 teaspoon dried basil

Salt and freshly ground black pepper to taste

About 2 pounds of fresh fish and shellfish, a combination of peeled and deveined shrimp; cooked lobster meat; and 1-inch cubes of swordfish, tuna, monkfish, or any firm-fleshed fish that will not flake when cooked

**Croutons**

6 slices French bread

1 tablespoon olive oil

1/4 cup freshly grated parmesan cheese

**Rouille**

1 egg yolk

1 teaspoon Dijon mustard

1 tablespoon red wine vinegar

3 garlic cloves, peeled

2 tablespoons chopped fresh basil

1 teaspoon chili powder

1 red bell pepper, roasted, peeled, and seeded

1/2 cup olive oil

1/4 cup fresh breadcrumbs

1. To prepare the stew, cook the bacon in a large saucepan until crisp. Add the onion, carrot, celery, and garlic. Sauté over medium heat, stirring frequently, for 5 minutes, or until the onion is translucent. Add the linguiça and cook 3 minutes. Add the tomatoes, orange zest, orange juice, wine, stock, parsley, thyme, and bay leaf. Bring to a boil and cook over medium heat until the liquid has reduced by one third, stirring occasionally. Add the basil. Bring back to a boil and season with salt and pepper.

2. While the stock is reducing, make the croutons. Brush the bread with the oil, then sprinkle generously with parmesan. Bake at 375°F. on a cookie sheet until the cheese is melted and the bread is crisp, about 10 minutes. Set aside.

3. To prepare the rouille, combine the first 7 ingredients in a blender or food processor fitted with a steel blade. Puree until smooth, then drizzle the olive oil very slowly into the mixture with the motor running. Add the breadcrumbs to thicken.

4. When ready to serve, heat the soup to boiling. Add the seafood and fish and bring back to a boil. Turn off the heat, cover the pot, and allow to sit for 5 minutes. Do not overcook the fish.

5. To serve, ladle the hot soup into bowls. Place a crouton in the center, and top with a few tablespoons of rouille.

*Note:* The soup base, croutons, and rouille can be prepared up to 2 days in advance and refrigerated, tightly covered. Bring the soup to a boil and cook the seafood just before serving.

*Sausage is one of the Portuguese influences on Nantucket cooking; perhaps the most common is the hearty Portuguese white bread made by bakeries such as Matt Fee's Something Natural. Back in the whaling days, the trade winds would push ships to the Azores and Cape Verde Islands before they could turn back toward their goal of rounding South America to reach the Pacific. The sailors who joined them returned to New England with their culinary heritage.*

*Molière wrote: "I live on good soup, not fine words."*

Scallops are one of the few reasons to look forward to winter on Nantucket, and their delicate, sweet flavor is what makes them such a treat. The creamed leeks accented with bits of smoky bacon make this scallop dish a comfort food consistent with the season. Serve the dish with steamed rice or mashed potatoes and a tossed salad.

*The English word scallop comes from the French escalope, which refers to the shell in which the mollusk lives.*

*If you have any of the creamed leeks left over, save them (or even freeze them) as an addition to mashed potatoes at some future time.*

## Sautéed Scallops with Leeks

[ Serves 6 ]

2 pounds bay scallops

2 tablespoons unsalted butter

9 leeks, white parts only, trimmed and cut into a fine julienne

2 garlic cloves, minced

2 cups heavy cream

1/2 pound bacon

Salt and freshly ground pepper to taste

1. Rinse the scallops, pat dry with paper towels, and set aside. Melt the butter in a skillet over low heat. Add the leeks and garlic and cook, covered, over low heat for 10 minutes, stirring occasionally. Add the cream, raise the heat to medium, and cook until the mixture is reduced by two thirds, stirring occasionally.

2. While the sauce is cooking, fry the bacon in a large skillet until crisp. Remove the bacon from the pan and crumble it. Add the bacon to the sauce and season the sauce with salt and pepper.

3. Discard all but 2 tablespoons of the bacon grease. Set the skillet over high heat, and when the bacon grease begins to smoke, add the scallops. Sauté, stirring frequently, for 2 minutes. Season the scallops with salt and pepper. To serve, divide the leek mixture among 6 plates, and top with the scallops.

*Note:* The leek mixture can be prepared 1 day in advance and refrigerated, tightly covered. Reheat it over low heat, but do not add the bacon or sauté the scallops until just before serving.

# Italian-Style Baked Bluefish

[ Serves 6 ]

3 pounds bluefish fillets

1/4 cup olive oil

2 celery stalks, trimmed and sliced

1 onion, peeled and diced

6 garlic cloves, minced

One 28-ounce can diced tomatoes, drained

1/2 cup dry white wine

1/4 cup chopped kalamata olives

4 tablespoons small capers, rinsed

2 tablespoons chopped parsley

2 teaspoons fresh thyme or 1/2 teaspoon dried thyme

Salt and freshly ground black pepper to taste

1. Skin the bluefish fillets by running the blade of a boning knife between the meat and skin. Remove the shallow layer of dark meat on the skin side of the fillets. Cut the fillets into 6 pieces, and refrigerate.

2. Heat the oil in a large skillet over medium heat. Add the celery, onion, and garlic. Sauté, stirring frequently, for 5 minutes, or until the onion is translucent. Add the tomatoes, wine, olives, capers, parsley, and thyme to the pan. Bring to a boil, reduce the heat to low, and simmer the sauce, partially covered, for 30 minutes, or until thick.

3. Preheat the oven to 375°F.

4. Layer half the sauce into a baking pan, and top with the bluefish fillets. Spoon the remaining sauce over the fish and bake the fish for 20 to 30 minutes, or until the fish flakes. Serve immediately.

*Note:* The sauce can be prepared 1 day in advance and refrigerated, tightly covered. Reheat it over low heat before baking the fish. Mackerel can be substituted for bluefish.

This is a bluefish recipe that's perfect for fall. It's homey and hearty, and the olive and tomato sauce pairs masterfully both in color and flavor with the fish. Serve it with some boiled rice or pasta and a tossed salad.

*Even if it's just a five-pound bluefish on your line, you think you're trying to reel in Moby Dick. Bluefish fight ferociously, which is why they are such a prized sports fish. While they swim off the coast of Nantucket all summer, their schools are most concentrated in mid-May when they arrive from the warmer waters off North Carolina and in October when they are beginning their southern swim.*

It's true; bluefish is very oily. However it's false that it's strong-tasting when it's cooked right out of the water. The oil in the fish keeps it naturally moist as it grills, as you'll taste in this easy recipe. Serve it with some oven-roasted potatoes and steamed asparagus.

*While it's against traditional wisdom, I find it easier to fillet fish starting at the head rather than the tail end. Cut around the gills and use the backbone of the fish as a guide. Slice along the backbone and you'll get the fillet off in one piece.*

# Grilled Bluefish
[ Serve 6 ]

3 pounds bluefish fillets

1/4 cup balsamic vinegar

1 cup dry white wine

3 tablespoons Dijon mustard

4 garlic cloves, minced

2 tablespoons minced parsley

1 tablespoon herbes de provence

Salt and freshly ground black pepper to taste

1/4 cup olive oil

1 cup mesquite or applewood chips

102

1. Skin the bluefish fillets by running the blade of a boning knife between the meat and skin. Remove the shallow layer of dark meat on the skin side of the fillets. Cut the fillets into 6 pieces.
2. Combine the vinegar, wine, mustard, garlic, parsley, herbes de provence, and salt and pepper in a plastic bag. Shake to combine. Add the olive oil and shake again. Add the bluefish and marinate, refrigerated, for 3 to 8 hours.
3. Light a charcoal or gas grill. Soak the mesquite chips in water to cover for 30 minutes. When the fire is hot, drain the wood chips and place them on the fire.
4. Drain the bluefish and place the fillets on the grill rack with what would have been the skin side down. Cover the grill and cook the fish for 6 to 8 minutes, or until it is opaque; there is no need to turn the fillets. Serve immediately.

*Note:* Mackerel can be substituted for the bluefish.

# Grilled Swordfish with Smoked Cheddar Sauce

[ Serves 6 ]

1/2 pound bacon, cut into small pieces

1/2 cup chopped onion

2 shallots, peeled and chopped

2 garlic cloves, minced

1 cup Chicken Stock (page 63)

1 cup heavy cream

2 teaspoons cornstarch

1 1/2 cups grated smoked Cheddar cheese

1 tomato, peeled, seeded, and finely chopped

Six 8-ounce swordfish steaks

Salt and freshly ground black pepper to taste

6 tablespoons your favorite fresh tomato salsa, for garnish

103

1. Light a charcoal or gas grill.

2. Cook the bacon in a skillet over medium-high until brown. Remove the bacon from the pan with a slotted spoon and pour off all but 2 tablespoons of the bacon fat. Add the onion, shallots, and garlic, and sauté over medium heat for 3 to 5 minutes, or until the onion is translucent, stirring occasionally. Add 3/4 cup of the stock and the cream. Bring to a boil, and simmer for 5 minutes. Mix the cornstarch with the reserved 1/4 cup of stock and stir it in. Stir the sauce over low heat until thickened and bubbly. Stir in the grated cheese and stir until melted. Add the tomato and reserved bacon bits and keep the sauce warm.

3. Sprinkle the fish steaks with salt and pepper and grill the fish for 2 to 4 minutes or each side, depending on thickness, or until the fish is still slightly translucent in the center

4. To serve, ladle some of the sauce into the center of a heated plate and top with a fish steak. Garnish with a mound of salsa

Note: The sauce can be prepared up to 2 days in advance and refrigerated, tightly covered. Reheat it in a saucepan over low heat, stirring frequently.

Smoked Cheddar cheese is a wonderful accent for swordfish steaks right off the grill. In addition to swordfish, I've served this sauce on most grilled fish, not to mention steaks and chicken breasts. Some wild rice and a steamed green vegetable make this a memorable meal.

If you have problems separating the strips of bacon, pull off the total number of slices, and place the whole block in the skillet. Within a few minutes the slices will soften and they'll be very easy to pull apart.

When sailing the Aegean, you know you're coming to an island by the aroma of fish grilling on the beach with its combination of herbs, garlic, and lemon. This treatment is a natural for Nantucket's local swordfish, and during the summer I'll serve this with Tomato and Mozzarella Salad with Oregano (page 45) and corn.

*George Brown Goode's History of the American Fisheries was a landmark book when it was published by the government in 1887. He writes that fishing for swordfish dates back to the 1840s on Nantucket. "Its flesh is excellent food, and it is captured by harpoon according an exciting and even dangerous sport. . . with the harpooner taking a position at the end of the bowsprit."*

## *Aegean Grilled Swordfish*
[ Serves 6 ]

Six 6-ounce swordfish steaks

1/3 cup freshly squeezed lemon juice

Grated zest from 1 lemon

6 garlic cloves, minced

1/4 cup chopped parsley

2 tablespoons dried oregano

1 tablespoon fresh thyme or 1 teaspoon dried thyme

1/2 cup olive oil

Salt and freshly ground black pepper to taste

104

1. Rinse the swordfish steaks and set aside. Combine the remaining ingredients in a heavy plastic bag and mix well. Add the fish steaks and marinate, refrigerated, for 2 to 3 hours.
2. Light a charcoal or gas grill.
3. When the fire is hot, remove the fish from the marinade, discarding the marinade. Grill the fish for 3 to 4 minutes on each side, or until slightly translucent in the center. Serve immediately.

*Note*: Other firm-fleshed fish such as sea bass, halibut, or scrod can be substituted.

# Indian-Style Sautéed Tuna

[ Serves 6 ]

Yogurt Sauce

1 pint non-fat yogurt, drained in a sieve
    for at least 3 hours

3 tomatoes, seeded and chopped

1 cucumber, peeled and chopped

3 garlic cloves, minced

3 scallions, trimmed and chopped

Salt and freshly ground black pepper to taste

Sautéed Tuna

Six 6-ounce tuna steaks, at least 1 inch thick

1/4 cup freshly squeezed lemon juice

4 garlic cloves, minced

1 tablespoon grated fresh ginger

1 jalapeño pepper, seeds and ribs removed,
    finely chopped

Salt and freshly ground black pepper to taste

1/2 cup olive oil

1 cup plain breadcrumbs

3 tablespoons ground cumin

1 tablespoon turmeric

*1.* To prepare the sauce, combine all the sauce ingredients and stir well. Refrigerate until ready to serve.
*2.* Rinse the tuna. Combine the lemon juice, garlic, ginger jalapeño, salt and pepper, and 1/4 cup of
the olive oil in a heavy plastic bag. Add the tuna and marinate, refrigerated, for 2 hours.
*3.* Combine the breadcrumbs, cumin, and turmeric on a plate. Remove the tuna from the marinade
and discard the marinade. Coat both sides of the fish with the breadcrumb mixture. Heat the remaining
1/4 cup olive oil in a large skillet over high heat. Add the fish and cook for 2 minutes on each side
for medium-rare. Serve with the yogurt sauce.

*Note:* The sauce can be prepared 1 day in advance and refrigerated, tightly covered.

Asian spices such as turmeric were part of the cache whaleboats would bring back to Nantucket from their journeys. Hearty tuna takes well to this assertive seasoning, and the delicious dish is cooled by the yogurt-based vegetable *raita*. Serve it with *naan* or flour tortillas.

*Prized bluefin tuna are caught in the waters off Nantucket during the summer months, since they love to eat bluefish and follow them north. During much of the summer they are farther north, off the coast of Maine, but local fishermen frequently nab them in late summer and early fall, when they're migrating back to warmer waters.*

Butter sauces, called *beurre blanc* in French, are wonderful for grilled fish since they moisten the fillets. This one also adds some assertive flavor and texture, with chilies and pecans as the stars.

*A vegetable peeler and a pair of tweezers are the best ways to get rid of those pesky little bones in fish fillets. Run a peeler down the center of the fillet, starting at the tail end. It will catch the larger pin bones, and a twist of the wrist pulls them out. For finer bones, use your fingers to rub the flesh lightly, and then pull out the bones with the tweezers.*

# Grilled Salmon with Spicy Pecan Butter

[ Serves 6 ]

Six 6- to 8-ounce salmon fillets

2 tablespoons olive oil

Salt and freshly ground black pepper to taste

1 jalapeño pepper, seeds and ribs removed

3/4 cup pecans, toasted in a 350°F. oven for 5 minutes

4 sprigs of parsley

4 sprigs of cilantro

1/4 pound (1 stick) unsalted butter, softened

2 tablespoons freshly squeezed lemon juice

1 1/3 cups dry white wine

4 shallots, peeled and finely chopped

1/3 cup half-and-half

106

1. Light a charcoal or gas grill.
2. Rub the salmon with olive oil, sprinkle the steaks with salt and pepper, and set aside. Combine the jalapeño, toasted pecans, parsley, cilantro, butter, and lemon juice in a food processor fitted with a steel blade and chop finely using the on and off pulsing action.
3. Place the wine and shallots in a small saucepan and reduce by half. Add the cream and reduce by half again. Slowly whisk in the pecan butter. Add salt and pepper to taste.
4. Grill the salmon for 10 minutes per inch of thickness.
5. To serve, top the grilled salmon with the butter sauce.

*Note:* The butter sauce can be made up to 4 hours in advance and kept hot in a warmed thermos bottle.

# Baked Cod with Tomatoes and Fennel

[ Serves 6 ]

1/4 cup olive oil

1 large onion, peeled and thinly sliced

3 garlic cloves, peeled and minced

2 fennel bulbs, cored and thinly sliced

One 28-ounce can diced tomatoes, drained

1 cup dry white wine

1/2 cup freshly squeezed orange juice

2 tablespoons Pernod

1 tablespoon grated orange zest

2 1/2 pounds thick cod fillets

Salt and freshly ground black pepper to taste

1. Preheat the oven to 450°F.
2. Heat the olive oil in a large saucepan over medium heat. Add the onion and garlic, and sauté, stirring frequently, for 3 minutes, or until the onion is translucent. Add the fennel and sauté 2 minutes. Add the tomatoes, wine, orange juice, Pernod, and orange zest to the pan. Bring to a boil, reduce the heat, and simmer, uncovered, for 5 minutes.
3. Transfer the vegetable mixture to a large baking dish. Sprinkle the fish with salt and pepper and place the fish on top of the vegetables. Bake for about 10 minutes, or until the fish is just slightly translucent in the center. Serve immediately.

*Note:* The vegetable mixture can be made 1 day in advance and refrigerated, tightly covered. Reheat it over low heat to a simmer before baking the fish.

Cod is one fish available year-round on Nantucket, and this Italian preparation is delectable, especially on cold fall and winter evenings. Any firm-fleshed white fish can be substituted, and all you need for accompaniments is some crusty garlic bread and a tossed salad.

*Some of my friends live on a low area beneath the bluffs of 'Sconset in an area dubbed Codfish Park. The original bluff village dates to the late 17th century, merely years after the first European settlement of the island. First built for whale watching, the crude shacks were occupied in the fall and spring by fishermen in search of cod. While most of the bluff houses were replaced by grander structures, the low-lying ones in Codfish Park—with mismatched additions known as "warts"—are now charming miniature homes.*

Scrod takes well to baking and poaching and does not suffer from missing a trip to the grill. The slight sweetness of the red onions accentuates the mild flavor of the fish, and some steamed or roasted new potatoes and sautéed spinach are excellent additions to complete the meal.

*Cod are so important to the history of New England fishing that Cape Cod became the official name for the sandbar. Cod are omnivorous, bottom-dwelling fish that are caught in both Nantucket Sound and in offshore waters.*

*Scrod is a fancier term for small cod, since the fillets are thinner and can be sautéed better than those taken from larger fish. In some restaurants, scrod can also be haddock, and the two are similar.*

# Sautéed Scrod with Red Onion Marmalade

[ Serves 6 ]

Six 6-ounce scrod fillets

Salt and freshly ground black pepper to taste

6 tablespoons (3/4 stick) unsalted butter

5 medium red onions, peeled and thinly sliced

3/4 cup dry red wine

1 teaspoon grated orange zest

2 tablespoons beach plum or red currant jelly

3 tablespoons olive oil

108

1. Season the fish fillets with salt and pepper and set aside.

2. Melt 3 tablespoons of the butter in a large skillet over medium heat. Add the onions, toss to coat, cover the pan, and cook over low heat for 10 minutes. Uncover the pan and cook the onions over medium heat until soft, about 15 minutes, stirring frequently. Add the wine, orange zest, and jelly and boil over medium-high heat until the liquid has almost evaporated. Season with salt and pepper and keep warm.

3. Heat the oil and 2 tablespoons of the butter in a frying pan over medium-high heat. When the butter foam begins to subside, sauté the fillets for 2 to 3 minutes on a side, turning them gently.

4. To serve, divide the onion mixture among 6 warmed plates, place the fish fillets on top, and top with the remaining butter.

*Note:* The onion mixture can be prepared 1 day in advance and refrigerated, tightly covered. Reheat it on very low heat. Sauté the fish just prior to serving.

109

# Reasons to Rise:
## Breakfast & Brunch Dishes

Chicken Hash is a specialty of the much-touted 21 Club in New York, and I was terribly disappointed when I tasted it. It was bland, though the concept was good. So I devised this recipe using grilled chicken to add innate flavor. It's also a great way to use up leftover grilled chicken.

*When onions caramelize and turn brown, the reaction is caused by the natural sugars in the vegetable. Adding a bit of granulated sugar speeds up the process.*

# Grilled Chicken Hash

[ Serves  6 ]

4 boneless and skinless chicken breast halves

1/3 cup olive oil

3 garlic cloves, minced

1 tablespoon herbes de provence

Salt and freshly ground black pepper to taste

4 tablespoons (1/2 stick) unsalted butter

2 large sweet onions, such as Vidalia or Bermuda, peeled and diced

1 teaspoon sugar

1 1/2 pounds redskin potatoes, scrubbed and quartered

1. Light a charcoal or gas grill.

2. Trim any fat off the chicken breasts and pound between 2 sheets of plastic wrap or wax paper to an even thickness of 1/2 inch using the flat side of a meat mallet or the bottom of a heavy skillet. Place 3 tablespoons of the olive oil in a mixing bowl and add the garlic, herbes de provence, and salt and pepper. Add the chicken breasts and marinate for 30 minutes. Grill the chicken breasts for 3 to 4 minutes on each side, or until cooked through. When cool, dice the chicken into 1/2-inch pieces and set aside.

3. Heat the butter and remaining olive oil in a large saucepan over low heat. Add the onions, toss to coat with the fat, and cover the pan. Cook over low heat for 10 minutes, stirring occasionally. Uncover the pan, raise the heat to medium, sprinkle with salt and stir in the sugar. Cook for 20 to 30 minutes, stirring frequently, until the onions are medium brown. If the onions stick to the pan, stir to incorporate the browned juices into the onions.

4. Place the potatoes in a saucepan and cover with cold water. Salt the water and bring the potatoes to a boil over high heat. Boil for 12 to 15 minutes, or until the potatoes are very tender when tested with a knife. Drain the potatoes and mash them roughly with a potato masher. Add the chicken and onions to the potatoes and mix well. Season with salt and pepper.

5. Preheat the oven to 450°F.

6. Spread the hash into a buttered 9 X 13-inch baking pan and bake for 15 minutes, or until the top is lightly brown. Serve immediately.

*Note:* The hash can be prepared 2 days in advance and refrigerated, tightly covered. Reheat it, covered with aluminum foil, for 10 minutes, then remove the foil and bake for 15 minutes more.

113

*This recipe also has the correct proportions for traditional corned beef hash. Substitute 1 1/2 pounds of corned beef, cut into 1/4-inch dice, for the chicken breasts.*

*According to John Mariani's **The Dictionary of American Food & Drink**, recipes for chicken hash date to the late 19th century.*

This hash—an ambrosial brunch dish for brisk fall and winter days—is as colorful as it is appetizing, with bright peppers and herbs adding aromatic interest to the sausage. Serve it with crisp oven-roasted potatoes and a tossed salad.

# Sausage and Pepper Hash
[ Serves  6 ]

2 pound bulk pork sausage

10 shallots, peeled and minced

6 garlic cloves, minced

3 yellow bell peppers, seeds and ribs removed, finely chopped

3 red bell peppers, seeds and ribs removed, finely chopped

3 green bell peppers, seeds and ribs removed, finely chopped

1 jalapeño pepper, seeds and ribs removed, finely chopped

1 tablespoon chopped fresh sage or 1 teaspoon dried sage

1 tablespoon fresh thyme leaves or 1 teaspoon dried thyme

1 tablespoon chopped fresh rosemary leaves or 1 teaspoon dried rosemary

2 teaspoons chopped fresh oregano or 1/2 teaspoon dried oregano

1/2 cup chopped parsley

3 bay leaves

Salt and freshly ground black pepper to taste

12 eggs

1. Place a large skillet over medium heat. Add the sausage, breaking up any lumps, and brown it well until no pink remains. Remove the sausage from the pan with a slotted spoon and set aside.

2. Add the shallots, garlic, yellow peppers, red peppers, green peppers, and jalapeño to the pan. Sauté the vegetables over medium heat for 3 minutes, or until the shallots are translucent. Return the sausage to the pan and add the sage, thyme, rosemary, sage, oregano, parsley, and bay leaves. Simmer the mixture over low heat for 20 to 30 minutes, or until the vegetables are very soft. Remove and discard the bay leaves. Tilt the pan and skim off as much grease as possible. Season the mixture with salt and pepper.

3. Preheat the oven to 350°F.

4. Spread the sausage mixture in a 9 X 13-inch baking dish. Make 12 indentations in the mixture with the back of a spoon and break 1 egg into each. Sprinkle the eggs with salt and pepper and bake for 12 to 15 minutes, or until the whites are set. Serve immediately.

*Note:* The sausage mixture can be made 2 days in advance and refrigerated, tightly covered. Reheat it over low heat or in a microwave oven before adding the eggs and baking the dish.

*Hash is a general term for food that is finely chopped. The English word first appears in the mid-17th century; it comes from the French word **hacher**, which means to chop. Since hash was frequently made with leftovers, inexpensive restaurants became known as "hash houses."*

This was one of the first recipes I devised; it dates to the early 1970s when I was teaching a course called "Budget Buffet" at the University of Cincinnati. It's great for a buffet brunch since the peppers become a one-dish meal.

*The rainbow of bell peppers now on the market is a relatively new phenomenon, and any brightly colored pepper can be substituted for another. Green peppers are immature red bell peppers; they are less expensive since they are not as perishable to ship. Green peppers have a harsher flavor than their brightly colored cousins.*

# Stuffed Brunch Peppers
[ Serves 6 ]

6 bell peppers of any color that can sit evenly when placed on a flat surface

2 tablespoons olive oil

1/4 cup Italian-flavored breadcrumbs

1 pound bulk sweet Italian sausage

1/2 cup spaghetti sauce

6 eggs

Salt and freshly ground black pepper to taste

3 tablespoons freshly grated parmesan cheese

*1.* Bring a large pot of salted water to a boil over high heat. Preheat the oven to 375°F.

*2.* Cut the tops off the peppers. Discard the tops and seeds and pull out the ribs with your fingers. Blanch the peppers in the boiling water for 4 minutes. Remove them from the water with tongs and place them upside down on paper towels.

*3.* Heat the olive oil in a skillet over medium heat. Add the breadcrumbs and sauté, stirring constantly, for 3 minutes, or until brown. Scrape the crumbs into a small bowl and set aside. In the same pan, cook the sausage over medium-high heat, breaking up lumps with a fork. Sauté the sausage for 5 minutes, stirring frequently, or until brown with no trace of pink. Remove the sausage from the pan with a slotted spoon and drain it on paper towels. Place the sausage in a small mixing bowl, and stir in the spaghetti sauce.

*4.* Place the peppers in a 9 X 13-inch oiled baking dish. Spoon the sausage mixture into the bottom of each pepper, dividing evenly. Break an egg on top of it and sprinkle the eggs with salt and pepper, the toasted breadcrumbs, and the parmesan. Bake for 20 minutes, or until the egg whites are set and the yolks are still slightly liquid. Serve immediately.

*Note:* The peppers can be prepared for cooking up to 2 hours in advance and kept at room temperature. Bake them just before serving.

# Springtime Quesadillas

[ Serves 6 ]

Vegetable oil spray or melted butter

Six 8-inch flour tortillas

4 ounces Boursin cheese with garlic
and herbs, softened

1 pound baked ham, thinly sliced

6 hard-boiled eggs, cut into 6 slices each

3 plum tomatoes, cored, seeded, and
thinly sliced

12 asparagus spears, cooked and cut into
2-inch sections

Freshly ground black pepper to taste

1 1/2 cups grated sharp Cheddar or
Gruyère cheese

1. Preheat the oven to 450°F. Cover 2 baking sheets with heavy-duty aluminum foil and spray the foil with vegetable oil spray or brush it with melted butter.

2. Place the tortillas on the baking sheets and spread the Boursin on half of each tortilla. Layer the ham, eggs, tomatoes, and asparagus on top of the cheese. Season with pepper and spread 1/4 cup of the Cheddar or Gruyère on each quesadilla. Fold the empty half of the tortilla over the filled side, pressing with the palm of your hand to seal them tightly. Spray the tops with vegetable oil spray or brush them with melted butter.

3. Bake the quesadillas for 5 minutes, turn them gently with a spatula, and bake for 4 to 5 minutes more, or until browned. Allow them to sit for 3 minutes, then cut each into 2 or 3 wedges. Serve immediately.

*Note:* The quesadillas can be prepared for baking up to 1 day in advance and refrigerated, tightly covered.

Here's a crunchy and creamy brunch dish that includes all the food groups you need for a balanced meal. You've got ham and eggs for protein, cheeses for calcium, and nutritious vegetables, all wrapped up in a tortilla. These can be served for brunch or cut into thirds as hors d'oeuvres for a brunch.

*Fresh asparagus should always be soaked before it's cooked to remove any sand that might be lingering in the tightly closed tip. When ready to cook the spears, break off the woody ends, then peel the bottom third of the stalks to remove the tough outer skin.*

I've often said that I would rather cook dinner for twenty than breakfast for two, which is why I often make a strata, since it has to be assembled well in advance so that the toast absorbs the custard mixture. This one combines two characteristic Nantucket ingredients, lobster and Portuguese sausage.

*You can create a strata with any combination of foods, as long as you keep the same proportions of bread, eggs, milk, and cheese. Any foods that you'd use to fill an omelet— from a Western with mixed vegetables and ham to herbed tomato—works for a strata.*

# Nantucket Strata

[ Serves 6 to 8 ]

12 slices good-quality white bread

4 tablespoons (1/2 stick) unsalted butter

1/2 red bell pepper, seeds and ribs removed, finely chopped

3 scallions, trimmed and chopped

1/4 pound bulk linguiça sausage

1/2 pound lobster meat, cut into 1/2-inch dice

2 cups milk

6 eggs

Salt and pepper to taste

1 cup grated Swiss cheese

1. Toast the bread and spread the slices with 2 tablespoons of the butter. Cut the bread into strips 1 inch wide and set aside.

2. Melt the remaining 2 tablespoons butter in a skillet over low heat. Add the red pepper and scallions and sauté for 3 minutes, stirring frequently. Scrape the mixture into a mixing bowl. Add the sausage to the skillet, breaking it up with a fork. Sauté over medium heat for 5 minutes, or until brown. Scrape the sausage into the bowl with the vegetables and stir in the lobster.

3. Whisk the milk and eggs together and add salt and pepper to taste. Arrange half the bread slices in a buttered 9 X 13-inch baking pan. Sprinkle with half the lobster mixture and half the cheese. Repeat with remaining bread, lobster, and cheese, and then pour the egg mixture over the top. Refrigerate the strata for at least 2 hours, or preferably overnight.

4. Preheat the oven to 350°F.

5. Cover the pan with foil and bake for 45 minutes. Remove the foil and bake for 10 minutes more, or until a knife inserted in the center comes out clean. Serve immediately.

*Note:* The strata can be assembled up to 2 days in advance and refrigerated, tightly covered. Crab or shrimp can be substituted for the lobster and Cheddar can be substituted for the Swiss cheese.

# Smoked Salmon Hash with Poached Eggs

[ Serves 6 ]

1/2 pound smoked salmon, cut into thin strips

1 small red onion, peeled and finely chopped

1/4 cup capers, drained and rinsed

1/3 cup sour cream

2 tablespoons horseradish

2 tablespoons Dijon mustard

3 tablespoons unsalted butter

2 tablespoons olive oil

1 1/2 pounds frozen hash-brown potatoes

12 eggs, cold

2 tablespoons distilled white vinegar

Salt and freshly ground black pepper to taste

1. Combine the smoked salmon, onion, capers, sour cream, horseradish, and mustard in a mixing bowl and set aside. Heat the butter and oil in a large skillet over medium-high heat. Add the potatoes and cook for 10 to 12 minutes, or until golden brown. Reduce the heat to low and stir in the salmon mixture. Cook, stirring gently, for 2 minutes, or until heated through. Season with salt and pepper.
2. While the potatoes are cooking, poach the eggs. Bring a saucepan of water to a simmer and add the vinegar. Break the eggs, one at a time, into a custard cup or saucer. Holding the dish close to the water's surface, slip the egg, into the water. Cook the eggs for 3 to 5 minutes, depending on desired doneness, keeping the water at just a bare simmer. Remove the eggs with a slotted spoon and place them in a bowl of cold water for 10 seconds to remove the vinegar and stop the cooking. Place the eggs gently on a kitchen towel to drain.
3. To serve, place a portion of hash onto each plate and top with 2 poached eggs.

Note: The hash can be prepared 3 hours in advance and reheated gently over low heat. If you are not serving the eggs immediately, leave them in the cold water for up to 3 hours. Reheat the eggs by holding them in simmering water in a slotted spoon for 20 seconds.

I learned how to make poached eggs in advance in the kitchen at the famed Commander's Palace in New Orleans, and after mastering their method I started devising dishes that used them without fear of spending my entire brunch in the kitchen. This hash is elegant, and incredibly easy to make since it uses frozen hash-brown potatoes.

If you're not sure about the freshness of your eggs, float them in a bowl of cold water. Eggs that are fresh will sink to the bottom of the bowl, since as eggs age air pockets form that cause them to float.

Savory pancakes are a great brunch dish, and these are distinctive since their base is wild rice. While I top them with smoked salmon, you can also use creamed chicken or fish. Do beware when frying the pancakes, since the wild rice has a tendency to pop like popcorn when it's fried.

*Wild rice, **zizania aquatica**, is native to North America, and it's not a species of rice at all. It's a grain grown on tall aquatic grasses, which must be harvested by hand. Select grains that are long and unbroken.*

*To serve these pancakes as an hors d'oeuvre, fry 1 tablespoon of batter for each pancake. It will make approximately four dozen tiny pancakes.*

# Wild Rice Pancakes with Smoked Salmon and Crème Fraîche

[ Serves 6 ]

3 eggs

1/4 cup minced shallots

2 garlic cloves, minced

1/2 cup all-purpose flour

3/4 cup heavy cream

3 cups cooked wild rice

Salt and freshly ground black pepper to taste

1/3 cup olive oil

3/4 cup crème fraîche

3/4 pound smoked salmon

6 tablespoons snipped chives

120

1. Preheat the oven to 275°F.

2. Whisk the eggs well, then whisk in the shallots, garlic, flour, cream, and wild rice. Season with salt and pepper. Heat the olive oil in a large skillet over medium heat. Add 1/4 cup of the batter and form it into an even pancake. Repeat with as many pancakes as will fit in the skillet. Cook for 4 to 5 minutes, or until the bottom is golden. Turn with a spatula and cook the other side for 3 minutes. Drain the pancakes on paper towels and keep them warm in the oven on a baking sheet. Repeat until all the batter is cooked, adding additional olive oil to the pan as needed.

3. To serve, spread crème fraîche on each of the warm pancakes and top with smoked salmon. Sprinkle the smoked salmon with the chives.

*Note:* The pancakes can be prepared 1 day in advance and refrigerated, tightly covered. Reheat them in a 300°F. oven, uncovered, for 8 to 10 minutes, or until warm.

# Summertime Baked Eggs

[ Serves 6 ]

1/4 cup olive oil

2 tablespoons unsalted butter

6 scallions, trimmed and thinly sliced

1 red bell pepper, seeds and ribs removed,
   chopped

1/2 pound mushrooms, wiped, stemmed,
   and thinly sliced

3 garlic cloves, minced

6 tomatoes, cored, seeded, and chopped

2 teaspoons herbes de provence

Salt and freshly ground black pepper to taste

12 eggs

1 1/2 cups grated Monterey Jack cheese

1. Preheat the oven to 350°F. Grease a 9 X 13-inch baking dish.

2. Heat the olive oil and butter in a skillet over medium heat. Add the scallions, red pepper, mushrooms, and garlic. Sauté for 3 minutes, stirring constantly. Add the tomatoes and herbes de provence, raise the heat to medium-high, and sauté for 5 minutes, or until the mixture has slightly thickened and the liquid has almost evaporated. Season the vegetables with salt and pepper.

3. Spread the vegetables in the baking dish in an even layer. Make 12 depressions in the vegetables with the back of a spoon and break an egg into each. Sprinkle the eggs with salt and pepper and then sprinkle the cheese over the top of the eggs and vegetables.

4. Bake for 12 to 15 minutes, or until the eggs are just set. Serve immediately.

*Note:* The vegetable mixture can be prepared 1 day in advance and refrigerated, tightly covered. Reheat it over low heat before adding the eggs and baking.

*I*'m always looking for more ways to use Nantucket's wonderful local tomatoes, and they join with sautéed vegetables to become a light and delicate base for this easy baked egg dish. Serve it with some crisp oven-roasted potatoes or hash-brown potatoes and a tossed salad.

*When buying mushrooms, it's best to choose loose ones rather than pre-packaged. Look for tightly closed mushrooms, since once the brown gills on the bottom are showing, they are past their prime. Store mushrooms in a paper bag rather than plastic, so they don't get mushy.*

There are few egg dishes that are as successful served at room temperature as they are hot, but this is one of them. Hearty and wholesome, this baked omelet is based on the *tortilla* served in small wedges at tapas bars in Spain.

*You can personalize this dish in many ways. Try adding some chopped ham or dry cured sausage, as well as different combinations of cheese.*

*Frittatas are Italian omelets, which are becoming increasingly popular here. They are an easy way to serve eggs to a crowd.*

# Spanish Frittata

[ Serves 6 ]

2 tablespoons olive oil

1 large potato, peeled and cut into 1/2-inch dice

1 red bell pepper, seeds and ribs removed, thinly sliced

1 sweet onion, such as Vidalia or Bermuda, peeled and thinly sliced

2 garlic cloves, minced

1 tablespoon fresh thyme leaves or 1 teaspoon dried thyme

8 eggs

1/4 cup freshly grated parmesan cheese

1/4 cup shredded mozzarella cheese

Salt and freshly ground black pepper to taste

2 tablespoons unsalted butter

1. Heat the olive oil in a skillet over medium-high heat. Add the potatoes and brown them well. Add the red pepper, onion, garlic, and thyme to the pan. Sauté, stirring constantly, for 3 minutes, or until the onion is translucent. Reduce the heat to low, cover the pan, and cook the vegetable mixture for 15 minutes, or until the vegetables are tender. Season with salt and pepper and let cool for 10 minutes.

2. Preheat the oven to 425°F.

3. Whisk the eggs well, stir in the parmesan and mozzarella cheese, and season the eggs with salt and pepper. Stir the cooled vegetable mixture into the eggs. Heat the butter in a large skillet over medium heat. Add the egg mixture and cook for 4 minutes, or until the bottom of the cake is lightly brown. Transfer the skillet to the oven and bake for 10 to 15 minutes, or until the top is brown.

4. Run a spatula around the sides of the skillet and under the bottom of the cake to release it. Slide it gently onto a serving platter, and cut it into wedges. Serve hot or at room temperature.

*Note:* The vegetable mixture can be prepared 1 day in advance and refrigerated, tightly covered. The frittata can be cooked up to 3 hours before serving.

# Vegetable Frittata with Pasta

[ Serves 6 to 8 ]

One 6-ounce package refrigerated
   angel hair pasta

3 tablespoons olive oil

2 small zucchini, trimmed and thinly sliced

4 scallions, trimmed and thinly sliced

3 garlic cloves, minced

2 tomatoes, cored, seeded, and finely chopped

3 tablespoons chopped basil

1 tablespoon chopped oregano

1/4 cup sliced green olives

6 eggs

1 cup freshly grated romano cheese

Salt and freshly grated black pepper to taste

3 tablespoons unsalted butter

*1.* Cook the pasta according to package directions until al dente. Drain and set aside to cool.

*2.* Heat the oil in a large skillet over medium-high heat. Add the zucchini, scallions, and garlic. Sauté for 3 minutes, stirring constantly, or until the zucchini is tender. Add the tomatoes, basil, oregano, and olives. Cook the mixture for 5 minutes, or until the liquid from the tomatoes has evaporated. Season with salt and pepper and cool for 10 minutes.

*3.* Preheat the oven to 425°F.

*4.* Whisk the eggs with the cheese and stir in the pasta and vegetables. Heat the butter in a large skillet over medium heat. Add the egg mixture and cook over medium heat for 4 minutes, or until the bottom of the cake is lightly brown. Transfer the skillet to the oven and bake for 10 to 15 minutes, or until the top is brown.

*5.* Run a spatula around the sides of the skillet and under the bottom of the cake to release it. Slide it gently onto a serving platter and cut it into wedges. Serve hot or at room temperature.

*Note:* The vegetable mixture and pasta can be prepared 1 day in advance and refrigerated, tightly covered. The frittata can be cooked up to 3 hours prior to serving.

In addition to serving this nutritious frittata at brunch, I also pack it to take on beach picnics since it can be served at room temperature. It's really a meal in itself.

*While we bake frittatas, the Italian word is derived from the Latin **frigere**, which means to fry.*

Quiches are the miniskirts of the food world. One year they're "in" and the next year they're "out." But in my kitchen they never fall from popularity, although my fillings tend to be more inventive than those of the classic French repertoire.

*The filling can also be used to make about four dozen mini quiches for hors d'oeuvres. Use the prebaked phyllo shells made by Athens Foods, found in the freezer section of supermarkets, and bake the mini quiches for 12 to 15 minutes, or until the tops are browned.*

# Herbed Sausage and Tomato Quiche

[ Serves 6 ]

One 9-inch pie shell, thawed if frozen

3/4 pound bulk pork sausage

3 garlic cloves, minced

2 shallots, peeled and minced

4 tomatoes, cored, seeded, and finely chopped

1 tablespoon herbes de provence

3 eggs

1 cup heavy cream

Salt and freshly ground black pepper to taste

1. Preheat the oven to 400°F.

2. Prick the pie shell all over with the tines of a fork and bake it for 8 to 9 minutes, or until the pastry is set and just starting to brown. Remove it from the oven.

3. Place a skillet over medium heat and crumble the sausage into it, breaking up any lumps with a fork. Cook the sausage for 5 minutes, stirring occasionally, until the sausage is brown with no pink remaining. Add the garlic and shallots and cook for 2 minutes. Add the tomatoes and cook for 5 to 7 minutes, or until the juice has evaporated. Cool the mixture for 10 minutes.

4. Reduce the oven temperature to 375°F. Whisk the eggs with the cream and season with salt and pepper. Stir in the sausage mixture, fill the pie shell, and bake the quiche for 25 to 30 minutes, or until it is browned and the eggs are set. Serve immediately.

*Note:* The sausage mixture can be prepared 1 day in advance and refrigerated, tightly covered. It does not need to be reheated, but do add 5 minutes to the baking time.

# Caramelized Onion Quiche

[ Serves 6 ]

One 9-inch pie shell, thawed if frozen

2 tablespoons unsalted butter

1 tablespoon olive oil

4 large onions, peeled and thinly sliced

Salt and freshly ground black pepper to taste

1 teaspoon sugar

3 eggs

1 cup heavy cream

1/2 cup grated Swiss or Gruyère cheese

*1.* Preheat the oven to 400°F.

*2.* Prick the pie shell all over with the tines of a fork and bake it for 8 to 9 minutes, or until the pastry is set and just starting to brown. Remove it from the oven.

*3.* Heat the butter and oil in a large saucepan over low heat. Add the onions, toss to coat with the fat, and cover the pan. Cook over low heat for 10 minutes, stirring occasionally. Uncover the pan, raise the heat to medium, sprinkle with salt and stir in the sugar. Cook for 30 to 40 minutes, stirring frequently, until the onions have turned dark brown. If the onions stick to the pan, stir to incorporate the browned juices into the onions. Cool the onions for 10 minutes.

*4.* Reduce the oven heat to 375°F. Whisk the eggs with the cream and stir in the cheese and cooled onions. Season with salt and pepper and pour the mixture into the partially baked pie shell. Bake the quiche for 25 to 30 minutes, or until it has browned and the eggs are set. Serve immediately.

*Note:* The onions can be prepared 2 days in advance and refrigerated, tightly covered. They do not need to be reheated, but do add 5 minutes to the baking time.

*If* I had to choose a favorite vegetable ingredient it would be sweet caramelized onions. I love onion soup; I add the onions to mashed potatoes; and I use them to flavor this easy to prepare quiche.

*The filling can also be used to make about four dozen mini quiches for hors d'oeuvres. Use the prebaked phyllo shells made by Athens Foods, found in the freezer section of supermarkets, and bake the mini quiches for 12 to 15 minutes, or until the tops are browned.*

*Onions are much easier to slice and dice if you start by cutting them in half through the root end. That way the halves sit firmly on your cutting board.*

Alas, by December the fruit selection is rather bleak; this hot, homey compote, however, is a welcome addition to any breakfast or brunch. It combines winter pears with a selection of dried fruit for a succulent accent. It also goes well with roast turkey or pork at dinnertime.

*Hot fruit dishes such as this one are part of the colonial heritage, especially in the South. In communities such as Williamsburg, Virginia, the pineapple was a symbol of welcome and hospitality, and a cauldron of fruit was included at many meals or as a welcome snack when guests arrived.*

# Christmas Stroll Fruit Compote

[ Serves 6 to 8 ]

2 cups cranberry juice

1/2 cup sugar

1/4 cup crème de cassis

1 tablespoon grated orange zest

2 teaspoons grated lemon zest

1 cinnamon stick

2 tablespoons unsalted butter

3 large ripe pears, peeled and cut into 1 1/2-inch dice

1/2 cup dried apricots, halved

1/2 cup dried cranberries

2 tablespoons freshly squeezed lemon juice

126

1. Combine the cranberry juice, sugar, crème de cassis, orange zest, lemon zest, and cinnamon stick in a saucepan. Bring to a boil over medium-high heat, reduce the heat, and simmer for 5 minutes. Add the butter, pears, dried apricots, and dried cranberries. Simmer the fruit mixture for 15 to 20 minutes, or until the pears are tender. Remove the fruit from the pan with a slotted spoon and discard the cinnamon stick.
2. Boil the liquid until it is reduced to 1 cup. Return the fruit to the pan, and stir in the lemon juice. Serve hot or at room temperature.

*Note:* The fruit compote can be prepared 3 days in advance and refrigerated, tightly covered. Reheat it over low heat before serving.

# Potato Pancakes

[ Serves  6 to 8 ]

1/2 pound onions, peeled and diced

2 eggs

1/2 cup all-purpose flour

Salt and freshly ground black pepper to taste

1 pound potatoes, peeled and cut into
   1-inch cubes

1 1/2 cups vegetable oil

---

*1.* Preheat the oven to 300°F.

*2.* Place the onions, eggs, flour, and salt and pepper in the workbowl of a food processor fitted with a steel blade. Puree until smooth. Add the potatoes and pulse until the potatoes are finely chopped but not pureed.

*3.* Heat 1 cup of the oil in a skillet over medium-high heat to a temperature of 375°F. Stir the potato mixture. Add by 1/4 cup measures, being careful not to crowd the pan. Cook for 4 minutes, or until the bottom is browned. Carefully turn the pancakes with a slotted spatula and cook for 4 to 5 minutes on the other side. Remove the pancakes from the skillet, and drain on paper towels. Place cooked pancakes on a baking sheet and keep them warm in the oven with the door ajar.

*4.* Skim the oil with a slotted spoon. Add more oil as necessary and cook the remaining pancakes as directed. Serve immediately.

*Note:* The batter can be made up to 3 hours in advance. Press a sheet of plastic wrap directly into the surface of the mixture to prevent discoloration. Refrigerate until ready to fry.

*I* grew up in New York, where potato *latkes* were a favorite food in local delis. The food processor has eased preparation of many dishes, including potato pancakes. These can be served as a side dish to a breakfast or brunch entree or as a pancake topped by another food.

*If serving the pancakes topped with a sweet food such as applesauce, omit the pepper from the recipe.*

*You can use sweet potatoes or yams for this recipe instead of white potatoes. The pancakes will have a glowing orange color and a slightly sweet flavor.*

# Accessories that Star:

## Side Dishes

Garlicky gazpacho is a staple of summer soups, and this refreshing salad utilizes all the same ingredients and flavors. Take it on picnics or serve it with any simple grilled or broiled entree.

*It's easier to slice and dice bell peppers from the inside out. Once the seeds and ribs have been removed, place the shiny, slippery skin on your cutting board. You'll find it's easier to control your knife and cut the size pieces you desire.*

## Gazpacho Salad

[ Serves 6 ]

1 sweet onion, such as Vidalia or Bermuda, peeled and diced

2 cucumbers, peeled, seeded, and cut into 1/2-inch dice

1 green bell pepper, seeds and ribs removed, cut into 1/2-inch dice

1 red bell pepper, seeds and ribs removed, cut into 1/2-inch dice

6 medium tomatoes, cored, seeded, and cut into 1/2-inch dice

5 garlic cloves, minced

1 jalapeño pepper, seeds and ribs removed, finely chopped

1/4 cup sherry vinegar

Salt and freshly ground black pepper to taste

1/3 cup extra virgin olive oil

1/4 cup chopped cilantro leaves

130

1. Place the onion, cucumber, green pepper, red pepper, and tomatoes in a mixing bowl. Combine the garlic, jalapeño, vinegar, and salt and pepper in a jar with a tight-fitting lid and shake well. Add the olive oil and cilantro and shake well again.

2. Pour the dressing over the salad and refrigerate for 2 to 4 hours, tightly covered. Serve chilled.

*Note:* The salad should not be made more than 8 hours in advance.

# Celery Seed Slaw

[ Serves 6 to 8 ]

1/3 cup vegetable oil

1/2 cup sugar

1/2 cup cider vinegar

1 tablespoon celery seeds

1 tablespoon dry mustard

Salt and freshly ground black pepper to taste

One 2-pound head of green cabbage, cored and shredded

1 small red onion, peeled and thinly sliced

1 green pepper, seeds and ribs removed, thinly sliced

1 red bell pepper, seeds and ribs removed, thinly sliced

1. Combine the oil, sugar, and vinegar in a small saucepan and bring to a boil over medium heat, stirring occasionally. Reduce the heat to low and stir in the celery seed, mustard, and salt and pepper. Simmer for 2 minutes.

2. Combine the cabbage, onion, green pepper, and red pepper in a large mixing bowl. Toss the dressing with the salad. Allow the slaw to sit at room temperature for 2 hours, tossing it occasionally. Refrigerate the slaw for 4 to 6 hours. Drain it well before serving.

*Note:* The salad can be made 1 day in advance and refrigerated, tightly covered with plastic wrap.

*This is my signature cole slaw, and it's very low in calories since it contains no mayonnaise. It's a crunchy sweet-and-sour slaw that's flavored with sharp mustard and tasty celery seed, and it goes with anything from simple sandwiches to grilled lobsters.*

*Cole slaw has been part of American cooking since the 18th century. The name of the dish comes from the Dutch word **koolsla**, which means cabbage salad.*

Shredded red cabbage that's slightly steamed becomes the basis for this great winter salad alternative. I serve it along with smoked meats or as a salad appetizer. You can top it with some pieces of grilled chicken, pork, or seafood and serve it as a light lunch or supper.

*Choose heads of cabbage that are tightly closed and feel heavy for their size. Cabbage is a resilient vegetable, which is why it was used extensively before refrigeration. It can be stored for up to three weeks, refrigerated.*

# Red Cabbage Slaw

[ Serves 6 ]

One 1 1/2-pound red cabbage, cored and shredded

2 carrots, peeled and coarsely grated

1/2 red onion, peeled and thinly sliced

2 tablespoons grated fresh ginger

3/4 cup cider vinegar

3 tablespoons honey

3 tablespoons vegetable oil

Salt and freshly ground black pepper to taste

1/2 cup golden raisins

3 scallions, trimmed and thinly sliced

132

1. Place the cabbage, carrots, and red onion in a vegetable steamer set over boiling water. Steam for 5 minutes, drain, and place the vegetables in a mixing bowl. Combine the ginger, vinegar, honey, oil, and salt and pepper in a jar with a tight-fitting lid. Shake well and pour the dressing over the steamed vegetables. Marinate at room temperature for 2 hours, stirring occasionally.

2. Plump the raisins in boiling water for 15 minutes. Drain and add them to the salad. Place the salad in a colander set over another mixing bowl. Drain the vegetables, pressing with the back of a spoon to extract as much liquid as possible.

3. Place the juice in a small saucepan and boil it over medium-high heat until only 1/2 cup remains. Stir the reduced dressing back into the salad along with the scallions. Chill the salad for at least 1 hour before serving.

*Note:* The salad can be made up to 1 day in advance and refrigerated, tightly covered.

# Caponata

[ Serves 6 to 8 ]

One 1-pound eggplant, peeled and cut into 1/2-inch cubes

Salt and freshly ground black pepper

1/3 cup olive oil

2 celery stalks, trimmed and diced

1 onion, peeled and diced

4 garlic cloves, minced

1/4 cup red wine vinegar

1 teaspoon sugar

One 15-ounce can diced Italian plum tomatoes

1 tablespoon tomato paste

6 large green olives, pitted, slivered, and well rinsed

2 tablespoons small capers, drained and rinsed

2 tablespoons anchovy paste (optional)

1. Place the eggplant in a colander and sprinkle liberally with salt. Place a plate on top of the eggplant cubes and weight the plate with cans. Place the colander in a sink or on a plate and allow the eggplant to drain for 30 minutes. Rinse the eggplant cubes and pat dry on paper towels.

2. Heat half the olive oil in a skillet over medium heat. Add the celery and sauté for 3 minutes. Add the onion and garlic and sauté for 3 minutes more, or until the onion is translucent. Remove the vegetables from the pan with a slotted spoon.

3. Pour the remaining olive oil into the skillet and sauté the eggplant cubes over medium-high heat, stirring and turning them constantly for about 6 minutes, or until they are lightly browned. Return the celery mixture to the skillet and add the vinegar, sugar, tomatoes, tomato paste, olives, capers, and anchovy paste. Bring to a boil, reduce the heat, and simmer, uncovered, stirring frequently, for about 15 minutes, or until the vegetables are cooked but still retain texture. Adjust the seasoning and serve at room temperature or chilled.

*Note:* The caponata can be made 2 days in advance and refrigerated, tightly covered.

This classic Italian dish is extremely versatile. It can be served at any temperature and glamorizes a simple grilled entree. It can also be served as an appetizer or as part of an antipasto buffet. The silky eggplant and crunchy celery are augmented with salty capers and olives in a hearty tomato sauce.

*Like many recipes, this one calls for one tablespoon of tomato paste. I buy tomato paste that comes in a tube; it will keep refrigerated for a few weeks. If you must open a can, then freeze the rest in one-tablespoon portions in an ice cube tray. Then store the small cubes in a heavy plastic bag.*

This spicy, crisp salad is a great diet dish for any Asian meal, since it has so much flavor and virtually no calories. The amount of red pepper determines how spicy it becomes, so you can tone it down to suit your taste.

If you're using English cucumbers for this salad, then just peel and slice them. The seeds are so small that it's not worth the time to scrape them out.

Not everyone is a fan of cucumbers. Samuel Johnson wrote that "a cucumber should be well sliced, and dressed with pepper and vinegar, and then thrown out, as good for nothing."

# Thai Cucumber Salad

[ Serves 6 ]

3/4 cup distilled white vinegar

1/4 cup (firmly packed) light brown sugar

1 tablespoon Thai or Vietnamese fish sauce

1 to 2 teaspoons crushed red pepper

3 cucumbers, peeled, halved, seeded, and thinly sliced

3 plum tomatoes, cored, seeded, and diced

*1.* Combine the vinegar, brown sugar, fish sauce, and red pepper in a heavy plastic bag. Mix well to dissolve the sugar. Add the cucumbers and marinate for two hours, refrigerated. Add the tomatoes, and marinate an additional 20 minutes. Drain the salad from the marinade, and serve chilled.

*Note:* The salad can be made up to 2 days in advance and refrigerated, tightly covered.

# Sautéed Spinach with Garlic

[ Serves 6 ]

3 tablespoons olive oil

2 pounds spinach, stemmed, rinsed, and drained

3 garlic cloves, minced

1/4 cup freshly grated parmesan cheese

Salt and freshly ground black pepper to taste

*1.* Heat 1 tablespoon of the olive oil in a large skillet over medium-high heat. Add a few handfuls of spinach and sauté until it begins to wilt. Continue adding the spinach until it has all wilted. Drain the spinach, pressing with the back of a spoon to extract as much liquid as possible.

*2.* Heat the remaining olive oil in a skillet over medium heat. Add the garlic and sauté for 2 minutes, stirring constantly. Add the spinach and heat it through. Sprinkle with the parmesan cheese and stir to melt the cheese. Season with salt and pepper to taste. Serve immediately.

*Note:* The spinach can be sautéed up to 8 hours in advance. Sauté the garlic and reheat the spinach just before serving.

*I*'m sure you've noticed by now that I am very fond of garlic and that I use it for just about every savory dish. This is a classic Italian way of cooking bright green, nutritious spinach, and the garlic perks up the flavor.

*While many supermarkets now stock spinach that they claim has been washed three times, I'm still suspicious and wash it again. The best way to wash spinach is to fill a large mixing bowl with cold water, add the spinach leaves, and bob them up and down in the water. Remove the leaves from the top of the bowl; the grit will have settled to the bottom.*

This flavorful mélange
of vegetables, similar to
French ratatouille, is like a
quiche without the crust.
It's as good cold as it is
hot, and I've cut it into
small rounds and served
it on crackers or slices
of cucumber as an
hors d'oeuvre.

## Summer Vegetable Custard

[ Serves 6 ]

One 1-pound eggplant, cut into 1/2-inch dice

Salt and freshly ground black pepper to taste

1/4 cup olive oil

3 onions, peeled and diced

4 garlic cloves, minced

1 red bell pepper, seeds and ribs removed
   cut into 1/2-inch dice

2 small zucchini, trimmed and cut into
   1/2-inch dice

4 plum tomatoes, cored, seeded, and cut
   into 1/2-inch dice

2 tablespoons chopped fresh basil or
   1 teaspoon dried basil

1 tablespoon fresh thyme leaves or 1/2
   teaspoon dried thyme

6 eggs

1/4 cup sour cream

*1.* Place the eggplant in a colander and sprinkle liberally with salt. Place a plate on top of the eggplant cubes and weight the plate with cans. Place the colander in a sink or on a plate and allow the eggplant to drain for 30 minutes. Rinse the eggplant cubes and pat dry on paper towels.

*2.* Heat the olive oil in a large skillet over medium heat. Add the onions and garlic and sauté, stirring frequently, for 3 minutes, or until the onions are translucent. Add the eggplant, red pepper, zucchini, tomatoes, basil, and thyme to the pan. Sauté for 5 minutes, stirring frequently.

Reduce the heat to low, cover the pan, and cook the vegetables for 20 minutes, or until they are soft and the liquid has almost evaporated. Season with salt and pepper, and let cool 10 minutes.

*3.* Preheat the oven to 350°F. Oil a 9 X 13-inch baking dish.

*4.* Whisk the eggs with the sour cream and salt and pepper. Stir the eggs into the vegetable mixture and pour it into the prepared pan. Bake the custard for 45 minutes, or until the eggs are set and the top is lightly browned. Serve hot, at room temperature, or chilled.

*Note:* The custard can be made 1 day in advance and refrigerated, tightly covered, if it is to be served chilled. Do not reheat it.

*Feel free to change this recipe to utilize whatever vegetables look best at your market. Yellow squash can be substituted for zucchini, and any color of bell pepper works well. You can also use fresh oregano or thyme instead of the basil.*

A few years ago I spent three months traveling in the Southwest to film the *Great Chefs of the West* television series. This salad is based on one created for that series by Dallas-based cookbook author Anne Lindsay Greer. It's a colorful and flavorful accompaniment to any grilled meal.

138

# Black Bean and Papaya Relish

[ Serves 6 ]

Black Beans

1/2 cup dried black beans, rinsed and picked over

1 cinnamon stick

2 garlic cloves, minced

1/2 teaspoon freshly ground black pepper

Papaya Salad

1 ripe papaya, peeled, seeded, and cut into 1/4-inch dice

1 medium jicama, peeled and cut into a 1/4-inch dice

1/2 red bell pepper, seeds and ribs removed, cut into 1/4-inch dice

1/4 cup chopped cilantro

Dressing

2 garlic cloves, minced

3 shallots, peeled and chopped

1/2 teaspoon ground cumin

2 tablespoons freshly squeezed lime juice

3 tablespoons sherry vinegar

1/3 cup freshly squeezed orange juice

Salt and cayenne to taste

1/4 cup olive oil

1. To prepare the beans, place the beans in a saucepan with water to cover by 2 inches. Add the cinnamon stick, garlic, and pepper to the water. Bring the beans to a boil over medium-high heat. Reduce the heat to low and simmer the beans, covered, 1 to 1 1/4 hours, or until they are tender but still retain their texture.  Drain the beans, discard the cinnamon stick, and chill well.

2. To prepare the salad, combine the beans with the papaya, jicama, red pepper, and cilantro in a mixing bowl.

3. To prepare the dressing, place the garlic, shallots, cumin, lime juice, vinegar, orange juice, and salt and cayenne in a jar with a tight-fitting lid. Shake well, then add the olive oil and shake well again.

4. Toss the salad with the dressing, and allow the salad to sit refrigerated for at least 20 minutes before serving.

*Note:* This salad can be made 1 day in advance.

*On Nantucket it's frequently hard to find ripe papayas, so I've made this dish with mangoes and even jarred mangoes. While it won't be as pretty, juicy, sweet, fresh pineapple can also be used. If you can't find jicama, you can use peeled apple. Toss it with the dressing first to prevent discoloration.*

*You can also make the salad with canned beans, if time is tight. Add a pinch of cinnamon and a bit more garlic to the dressing to compensate.*

This salad comes from my great love of Chinese leftovers. I realized that I preferred to eat Asian vegetable dishes cold the next day, rather than hot out of the wok. In addition to working well as a side dish with Asian foods, this salad can become a light meal with the addition of shrimp or cubes of chicken.

## Stir-Fried Vegetable Salad

[ Serves 6 to 8 ]

1/4 cup sesame seeds

1 bunch bok choy

1/2 pound snow peas

1/2 pound fresh shiitake mushrooms

2 tablespoons vegetable oil

2 tablespoons sesame oil

3 garlic cloves, minced

2 tablespoons finely minced ginger

4 scallions, trimmed and thinly sliced

1/2 cup oyster sauce

1/4 cup Chicken Stock (page 63)

2 tablespoons soy sauce

2 tablespoons dry sherry

*1.* Preheat the oven to 375°F.

*2.* Place the sesame seeds in a pie plate. Toast the seeds for 5 minutes, or until lightly browned. Remove the pan from oven and set aside.

*3.* Trim the root end off the bok choy and separate the head into ribs. Rinse the ribs under cold running water and pat dry with paper towels. Slice the ribs on the diagonal into 1/2-inch slices and set aside. Remove the tips from snow peas, rinse them in a colander, and set aside. Trim and discard the stems from the shiitake mushrooms. Wipe the mushroom caps with a damp paper towel and set the caps aside.

*4.* Heat the vegetable oil and sesame oil in a wok or large skillet over medium-high heat. Add the garlic, ginger, and scallions. Stir-fry 30 seconds, or until fragrant. Add the mushroom caps and stir-fry for 2 minutes, or until caps are soft. Add the bok choy and stir-fry for 1 minute. Add the snow peas and stir-fry for 1 minute. Add the oyster sauce, stock, soy sauce, and sherry. Stir well and bring to a boil. Boil for 1 minute, then remove pan from heat.

*5.* Using a slotted spoon, transfer the vegetables to a mixing bowl or serving dish. Serve at room temperature or refrigerate, tightly covered with plastic wrap, and serve chilled. Sprinkle the vegetables with the toasted sesame seeds just before serving.

*Note:* The salad can be prepared up to 2 days in advance and refrigerated, tightly covered.

*Store wild mushrooms, such as fresh shiitakes, in a paper bag rather than a plastic bag. Plastic causes mushrooms to become moist and soggy. An alternative method is to line a bowl with paper towels, add the mushrooms, then cover the bowl with more paper towels.*

Frozen green beans baked with canned cream of mushroom soup have been served for generations, and there's no question that the combination of beans and mushrooms is a great one. This creamy dish uses fresh vegetables, with just a touch of wine for added interest.

Most string beans today do not need to have the strings removed, since that trait has been bred out of most species. But some farm-fresh beans do need help. It's easy. Just snap off the stem end and use the stem to pull off the string.

# Green Beans with Mushroom Sauce

[ Serves  6 ]

1 1/2 pounds green beans, trimmed and cut into 1-inch pieces

3 tablespoons unsalted butter

2 shallots, peeled and chopped

2 garlic cloves, minced

1/2 pound fresh shiitake mushrooms, stemmed and sliced

1/2 cup marsala wine

1 cup heavy cream

Salt and freshly ground black pepper to taste

142

1. Bring a large pot of salted water to a boil over high heat. Add the green beans and cook for 4 minutes, or until just tender. Drain the beans and plunge them into a bowl of ice water. Drain when chilled and set aside.

2. Melt the butter in a skillet over medium heat. Add the shallots and garlic and sauté for 2 minutes. Raise the heat to medium-high and add the mushrooms. Sauté, stirring constantly, for 3 minutes, or until the mushrooms are tender. Raise the heat to high, add the marsala to the pan, and boil for 2 minutes, or until the liquid evaporates. Stir in the cream, reduce the heat to medium, and simmer for 3 minutes, or until reduced by one third.

3. Add the beans to the pan to reheat them in the hot sauce. Season with salt and pepper and serve immediately.

Note: The beans can be cooked and the sauce can be prepared 1 day in advance and refrigerated, separately, tightly covered. Reheat the sauce over low heat until simmering, then add the beans.

# Fall Tomato Gratin

[ Serves  6 ]

1/4 loaf French or Italian bread

1/3 cup olive oil

4 garlic cloves, minced

3 pounds tomatoes, cored, seeded, and
 cut into 1/2-inch dice

2 teaspoons chopped fresh oregano or
 1/2 teaspoon dried oregano

1 teaspoon thyme leaves or 1/4 teaspoon
 dried thyme

1/3 cup heavy cream

1/4 cup freshly grated parmesan cheese

Salt and freshly ground black pepper to taste

*1.* Preheat the oven to 375°F. Grease a medium gratin pan or baking dish.

*2.* Cut the bread into 1/2-inch cubes; you should have 3 cups. Heat the olive oil in a large skillet over medium heat. Add the garlic and sauté, stirring constantly, for 2 minutes, or until the garlic is fragrant. Add the bread cubes and sauté them, stirring frequently, for 3 to 4 minutes, or until they are light brown. Remove the pan from the heat and set aside.

*3.* Combine the bread cubes, tomatoes, oregano, thyme, cream, and salt and pepper in a mixing bowl. Toss to combine. Spread the mixture into the prepared dish and top with the parmesan cheese. Bake for 50 to 60 minutes, or until there is almost no liquid left in the gratin dish. Serve immediately.

*Note:* The gratin can be prepared for baking up to 6 hours in advance. Bake just before serving.

143

*Evenings on the island begin to get a bit chilly by mid-September, when there are still wonderful local tomatoes available. This hot gratin is a hearty dish, and the flavor of the fresh tomatoes emerges as the star.*

*I don't believe that it's worth the time to peel tomatoes. If you are a purist, then plunge the tomatoes into boiling water for 30 seconds, and the skins will slip off from the root end.*

*All it takes to seed tomatoes is to cut them in half and squeeze them gently over a sink or mixing bowl. I frequently save the seeds and juice and use them in stocks.*

The farms on Nantucket grow about six different kinds of cherry tomatoes, both red and orange. It's fun to mix them, as long as they're about the same size. While this dish is glorious in summer, I make it year-round using small red grape tomatoes during the winter months.

*Never cook tomatoes in an aluminum pan. It makes them lose their color, and it can impart a bitter undertaste.*

*If you want to serve this dish as a salad, just mound the tomatoes in the center of some leaves of Boston lettuce.*

# Sautéed Cherry Tomatoes

[ Serves 6 ]

3 pints cherry tomatoes

3 tablespoons olive oil

2 garlic cloves, minced

1/4 cup chopped basil

2 tablespoons chopped parsley

1 tablespoon thyme leaves or 1 teaspoon dried thyme

Salt and freshly ground black pepper to taste

*1.* Stem and rinse the cherry tomatoes. Heat the olive oil in a large skillet over medium heat. Add the garlic and sauté, stirring constantly, for 2 minutes, or until the garlic is fragrant. Add the tomatoes, basil, parsley, and thyme. Sauté for 2 minutes, or until the tomatoes are beginning to soften. Sprinkle with salt and pepper and serve immediately.

*Note:* The dish can be served hot or at room temperature. Do not reheat it.

# Ginger-Glazed Carrots

[ Serves 6 ]

1 1/2 pounds carrots, trimmed, peeled, and cut on the diagonal into 1/4-inch slices

3/4 cup freshly squeezed orange juice

3 tablespoons unsalted butter

3 tablespoons (firmly packed) dark brown sugar

2 tablespoons grated fresh ginger

1 teaspoon grated orange zest

2 scallions, trimmed and finely chopped

Salt and freshly ground black pepper to taste

1. Place the carrots, orange juice, butter, sugar, ginger, and orange zest in a large skillet. Bring to a boil over medium heat and cook the carrots, covered, for 4 minutes. Uncover the pan and simmer for 10 minutes, stirring occasionally, or until the liquid glazes the carrots and is almost evaporated.
2. Sprinkle the carrots with the chopped scallions, season with salt and pepper, and serve.

*Note:* The carrots can be prepared up to adding the scallions 2 days in advance and refrigerated, tightly covered. Reheat them, covered, over low heat and sprinkle with the scallions just before serving.

The principle of contrasting opposites extends from Chinese philosophy into Chinese cooking. In this dish, the sweetness of the carrots is balanced by zesty ginger and aromatic orange zest.

*Humorist Fran Lebowitz wrote that "carrots are acceptable as food only to those who lie in hutches eagerly awaiting Easter."*

These crisp and delicate pancakes can form a great base for grilled meats, fish, or poultry as well as being served as a side dish.

*Zucchini is Italian in origin and kept its native name when integrated into American cooking. Choose small zucchini since they tend to have a sweeter flavor, and the seeds are still tender, less pronounced.*

# Sautéed Zucchini Pancakes

[ Serves 6 ]

2 pounds zucchini

Salt and freshly ground black pepper to taste

2 eggs, lightly beaten

2 garlic cloves, minced

2 tablespoons chopped fresh basil or 1 teaspoon dried basil

1 cup Italian-flavored breadcrumbs

1/2 cup vegetable oil

146

1. Trim the ends off the zucchini and grate the zucchini through the largest holes of a box grater. Place the shreds in a colander and sprinkle liberally with salt. Allow the zucchini to drain over a mixing bowl for 30 minutes. Rinse well and then, using your hands, squeeze as much liquid as possible out of the zucchini. Set aside.

2. Preheat the oven to 200°F.

3. Combine the eggs, garlic, basil, and breadcrumbs in a mixing bowl. Stir in the zucchini and season with salt and pepper.

4. Heat 1/4 cup of the oil in a large skillet over medium-high heat. Add the zucchini mixture to the skillet in 1/4-cup mounds and flatten them to thin pancakes with the back of a spatula. Fry the pancakes for 2 to 3 minutes on each side, or until cooked through and lightly browned. Drain the pancakes on paper towels and keep them warm in the oven on a baking sheet. Repeat with the remaining mixture, adding more oil as necessary. Serve immediately.

*Note:* The zucchini mixture can be prepared 1 day in advance and refrigerated, tightly covered. Do not fry the pancakes until just before serving.

# Corn Pudding

[ Serves 6 ]

6 tablespoons (3/4 stick) unsalted butter, melted

5 eggs

1 1/2 cups half-and-half

1/4 cup all-purpose flour

3 cups fresh corn kernels, about 5 or 6 ears

4 scallions, trimmed and chopped

1/2 red bell pepper, seeds and ribs removed, finely chopped

2 garlic cloves, minced

2 tablespoons chopped parsley

2 teaspoons fresh thyme leaves or 1/2 teaspoon dried thyme

Salt and freshly ground black pepper to taste

1. Preheat the oven to 350°F. Butter a 2-quart soufflé dish or ovenproof casserole.
2. Whisk the eggs with the remaining butter, half-and-half and flour. Stir in the corn, scallions, red pepper, garlic, parsley, thyme, and salt and pepper.
3. Pour the mixture into the prepared dish and place the pudding in a roasting pan. Pour boiling water halfway up the sides of the dish. Bake for 45 minutes, or until the top is brown and a knife inserted in the center comes out clean. Allow to sit for 5 minutes before serving.

Note: The pudding can be prepared for baking up to 1 day in advance and refrigerated, tightly covered. The baking time should be increased by 10 minutes if the pudding is baked chilled.

While there's no way to beat eating fresh corn right off the cob, here is a recipe to dress up the kernels with colorful vegetables in a satiny custard. I cook extra corn while it's in season and freeze it, since this recipe is such a treat on winter tables.

Nantucket native Lucretia Mott was one of the country's first suffragettes. When she was not writing to advocate women's rights, she turned her pen to cooking. Discussing corn pudding, she wrote that "if the corn be young and milky, thee will not need so much milk."

This spiced red cabbage is my favorite winter vegetable. It pairs well with turkey for Thanksgiving and with meats ranging from roast pork to sautéed venison. The apple and jam add a bit of sweetness complemented by the aromatic cinnamon.

*Cabbage is one of the oldest vegetables in recorded history, although it's stature has ranged from lowly to esteemed depending on the culture. The philosopher Diogenes remarked to a young man: "If you lived on cabbage you would not be obliged to flatter the powerful." The retort was: "If you flattered the powerful you would not be obliged to live on cabbage."*

148

# Braised Red Cabbage

[ Serves 6 to 8 ]

One 2-pound red cabbage, cored and shredded

2 tablespoons red wine vinegar

2 tablespoons sugar

3 tablespoons unsalted butter

1 onion, peeled and chopped

1 McIntosh or Golden Delicious apple, peeled and chopped

1 cup dry red wine

1 cup Chicken Stock (page 63)

1 cinnamon stick

1 bay leaf

Salt and freshly ground black pepper to taste

1/3 cup beach plum or red currant jelly

*1.* Place the cabbage in a large bowl. Sprinkle with vinegar and sugar, and toss. Allow the cabbage to sit at room temperature for 1 hour.

*2.* Heat the butter in a large saucepan over medium heat. Add the onion and apple and sauté for 3 minutes, or until the onion is translucent. Add the wine, stock, cinnamon stick, and bay leaf. Bring to a boil and stir in the cabbage with any juices from the bowl.

*3.* Cover the pan and cook the cabbage over low heat for 30 to 45 minutes, or until the cabbage is tender. Discard the cinnamon stick and bay leaf and stir the jelly into the cabbage. Cook, uncovered, over medium heat for 10 minutes, or until the liquid reduces and becomes syrupy. Serve immediately.

*Note:* The cabbage can be prepared 2 days in advance and refrigerated, tightly covered. Reheat it over low heat, stirring occasionally.

# Maple-Glazed Beets

[ Serves 6 ]

2 bunches of beets

1/3 cup balsamic vinegar

1/4 cup maple syrup

2 tablespoons unsalted butter

2 tablespoons chopped parsley

Salt and freshly ground black pepper to taste

1. Preheat the oven to 425°F.

2. Cut off the beet greens, leaving 1 inch attached to the beets. Scrub the beets and wrap them in heavy-duty aluminum foil. Place the packet on a baking sheet and bake for 1 to 1 1/2 hours, or until the beets are tender. Unwrap the beets and when cool enough to handle, slip off the skins. Slice the beets into 1/4-inch slices and set aside.

3. Combine the vinegar, maple syrup, and butter in a large skillet. Bring to a boil over medium heat. Stir until the butter is melted, then add the beets and cook for 2 minutes, or until heated through. Sprinkle the beets with the parsley and season with salt and pepper. Serve immediately.

*Note:* The beets can be roasted 1 day in advance and refrigerated, tightly covered. Glaze them just before serving.

*Beets are innately sweet, and the combination of New England's prized maple syrup and heady balsamic vinegar make this a memorable and tasty winter vegetable dish. Any leftovers are wonderful additions to green salads.*

*Don't discard the beet greens. Cut them into thin slices and sauté them until crisp-tender in some butter.*

*Peel beets over a sheet of plastic wrap to avoid staining your counter. To remove the inevitable beet stains from your hands, wash them with lemon juice.*

This version of creamy squash puree updates the classic by using complex Chinese five-spice powder instead of cinnamon and sweet aromatic hoisin sauce in lieu of molasses. A staple for my Thanksgiving dinners, this colorful puree is also a luscious accompaniment for roast pork or chicken.

*Leftover puree can be turned into a soup by thinning it with milk and/or chicken stock until it has a soup consistency.*

*Acorn squash can be substituted for butternut squash, not only in this recipe but in any recipe. There is very little difference in the flavor or color.*

*When buying acorn or butternut squash, choose ones with dull skin. A shiny skin means that the squash was picked green.*

## Asian Butternut Squash Puree

[ Serves  6 ]

Two 1 1/2-pound butternut squash

1/3 cup freshly squeezed orange juice

3 tablespoons unsalted butter

1/2 cup hoisin sauce

1 teaspoon grated orange zest

1/2 teaspoon five-spice powder

Salt and freshly ground black pepper to taste

1. Preheat the oven to 350° F.

2. Cut the stems off the squash, and split them in half lengthwise. Place the squash, cut side down, in a baking pan and add 1 cup of water. Cover the pan with heavy-duty aluminum foil and bake the squash for 45 to 50 minutes, or until almost tender. Remove the squash from the pan, discard the water, and when cool enough to handle, scrape out and discard the seeds and scrape the pulp out of the shells.

3. Return the pulp to the pan, and add the orange juice, butter, hoisin sauce, orange zest, and five-spice powder. Cover the pan and bake the squash for 20 minutes more. Puree the squash in a food processor fitted with a steel blade or with an electric mixer. Season with salt and pepper and serve immediately.

*Note:* The squash can be prepared 2 days in advance and refrigerated, tightly covered. Reheat it, covered, over low heat, stirring occasionally.

# Stewed Beans à la Cavedon

[ Serves 6 ]

1/3 cup olive oil

4 garlic cloves, minced

1 large red onion, peeled, halved, and thinly sliced

6 anchovy fillets, finely chopped

2 tablespoons chopped parsley

Two 15-ounce cans white beans, preferably Stewart brand, drained and rinsed

1/2 cup water

Pinch of ground cinnamon

2 tablespoons red wine vinegar

Freshly ground black pepper to taste

1 cup chopped tomatoes, for garnish

*1.* Heat the olive oil in a saucepan over medium heat. Add the garlic and onion and sauté, stirring frequently, for 3 minutes, or until the onion is translucent. Add the anchovies, parsley, beans, water, and cinnamon to the pan. Simmer the beans, uncovered, over low heat for 15 minutes, adding more water if the liquid has evaporated.

*2.* Stir the vinegar into the beans and season them with pepper. Serve the beans hot, with chopped tomato sprinkled on top.

*Note:* The beans can be prepared 2 days in advance and refrigerated, tightly covered. Reheat them over low heat or in a microwave oven.

My friend Suzanne Cavedon's great-grandmother brought this bean recipe with her from Venezia, in northern Italy. I have fond memories of eating this dish with fresh corn, tomatoes, and skewers of grilled chicken at Suzanne's Codfish Park cottage on starry August nights.

*Jazz great Louis Armstrong used to sign his letters: "Red beans and ricely yours."*

The best aïoli sauce I've ever tasted was in Provence, where it was used as the dressing for a colorful potato salad. Every time I taste a garlicky bite of this dish I see fields of sunflowers and hillsides of lavender.

*I boil potatoes whole for salads since they retain their shape better that way. If you don't want to take the time, there is a way that diced potatoes can retain their shape: Add some white distilled vinegar to the salted water.*

*I usually make a double batch of the aïoli sauce, since it's a wonderful condiment for cold seafood and poultry.*

# Garlicky Potato Salad

[ Serves 6 ]

2 pounds small redskin potatoes, scrubbed

One 1-pound bag frozen peas and carrots

1 red bell pepper, seeds and ribs removed, finely chopped

Aïoli Sauce

6 garlic cloves, peeled

2 egg yolks, at room temperature

3/4 cup extra virgin olive oil

1 tablespoon freshly squeezed lemon juice

Salt and freshly ground black pepper to taste

152

*1.* Place the potatoes in a saucepan and add cold water to cover. Salt the water and bring the potatoes to a boil over high heat. Boil them for 10 to 20 minutes, or until tender. Drain the potatoes. When cool enough to handle, cut them into bite-size pieces and place them in a large mixing bowl. Chill well.
*2.* Cook the peas and carrots according to package directions and add them to the bowl with the potatoes to chill. Add the red pepper to the bowl.
*3.* To prepare the aïoli sauce, combine the garlic cloves and egg yolks in a food processor fitted with a steel blade or in a blender. Puree, then very slowly add the olive oil through the feed tube of the food processor or the top of the blender. When the sauce has emulsified and thickened, add the lemon juice and season the sauce with salt and pepper.
*4.* Combine the sauce with the salad and serve chilled.

*Note:* The salad can be made 1 day in advance and refrigerated, tightly covered.

# Janet's Fourth of July Potato Salad

[ Serves 6 ]

2 pounds small redskin potatoes, scrubbed

1 cucumber, peeled

1 green bell pepper, seeds and ribs removed

1 small red onion, peeled

3 celery stalks, trimmed

1/2 cup Miracle Whip salad dressing

Salt and freshly ground black pepper to taste

1. Place the potatoes in a large saucepan of cold water. Salt the water, bring the potatoes to a boil, and boil the potatoes for 10 to 20 minutes, or until they are cooked through. Drain the potatoes and chill well. Cut the potatoes into 1-inch cubes and place them in a large mixing bowl.

2. Cut the cucumber in half lengthwise and scrape out the seeds with a teaspoon. Slice the cucumber into thin arcs, and add to the potatoes. Cut the green pepper into 1-inch sections and slice each section into thin strips. Add to the mixing bowl. Cut the onion in half through the root end, and cut each half into thirds. Cut into thin slices and add to the mixing bowl. Cut each celery stalk in half lengthwise and thinly slice the celery. Add to the mixing bowl.

3. Toss the potato salad with the Miracle Whip and season with salt and pepper to taste. Serve well chilled.

*Note:* If using mayonnaise instead of Miracle Whip, add 2 tablespoons of red wine vinegar to the salad. The salad can be made 1 day in advance and refrigerated, tightly covered.

*I clamor for invitations to my friend Janet Morell's house for any meal. She's a great cook, and this simple potato salad is crunchier than most since it includes many colorful fresh vegetables.*

*Janet makes the cucumber more attractive by running a table fork down the length of it, creating small flutes before seeding and slicing it.*

*A way to keep onions from overpowering other ingredients in a salad after a few hours is to soak the cut onions for about 10 minutes in a bowl of cold water with a few table-spoons of vinegar added.*

Many people ask how I come up with concepts for recipes, and this dish is an example of my method. I had leftover oven-roasted potatoes in the refrigerator and wanted to take them on a picnic. So they became a salad. The result was so appealing that I started experimenting to create a crisp potato salad when there are no leftovers.

*Instead of dropping potatoes into cold water to prevent them from browning, you can just wrap them in some layers of damp paper towels.*

# Hash-Brown Potato Salad with Bacon and Onion

[ Serves 6 ]

1 1/2 pounds boiling potatoes, quartered
  lengthwise and cut crosswise into 1-inch slices

1/4 pound bacon, cut into 1/2-inch slices

2 tablespoons vegetable oil

1 tablespoon mustard seeds

1 tablespoon chopped fresh rosemary
  or 1 teaspoon dried rosemary

3 tablespoons cider vinegar

1/2 red onion, peeled and finely chopped

1 celery stalk, trimmed and thinly sliced

1/3 cup mayonnaise, or to taste

2 tablespoons chopped parsley

Salt and freshly ground black pepper to taste

154

1. Steam the potatoes in a steamer set over boiling water, covered, for 6 to 8 minutes, or until they are barely tender. Remove the potatoes from the steamer and set aside.

2. Cook the bacon over medium-high heat until crisp. Remove the bacon from the pan with a slotted spoon, drain it on paper towels, and discard all but 2 tablespoons of the fat. Add the oil to the skillet, heat over medium heat, and fry the mustard seeds, partially covered, for 10 seconds, or until they stop popping. Add the potatoes and the rosemary and cook the mixture, turning the potatoes carefully, for 10 minutes. Add 2 tablespoons of the vinegar and cook the potatoes, turning carefully, for 5 minutes, or until they are crusty and golden.

3. Transfer the potatoes to a large bowl and let them cool. Add the onion and celery to the potatoes. Thin the mayonnaise with the remaining 1 tablespoon vinegar, add it to the salad with the bacon, parsley, and salt and pepper to taste, and toss the salad. Serve the salad at room temperature.

*Note:* The salad can be made 1 day in advance and refrigerated, tightly covered. Allow the salad to come back to room temperature before serving.

# Sweet Potato Salad with Mustard Dressing

[ Serves 6 to 8 ]

2 pounds sweet potatoes, scrubbed, quartered lengthwise, and cut into 2-inch pieces

3 tablespoons white wine vinegar

2 tablespoons Dijon mustard

Salt and freshly ground black pepper to taste

1 shallot, finely chopped

2 garlic cloves, minced

1/2 cup olive oil

1/4 cup finely chopped red onion

1/4 cup finely chopped red bell pepper

1/4 cup finely chopped cornichons or sweet pickle slices

1. Place the sweet potatoes in a saucepan and cover with cold water. Salt the water and bring the potatoes to a boil over high heat. Boil for 10 minutes, or until the potatoes are tender. Drain well and peel the potatoes when cool enough to handle. Cut the potatoes into bite-size pieces, and place them in a mixing bowl.

2. Combine the vinegar, mustard, salt and pepper, shallot, garlic, and oil in a jar with a tight-fitting lid and shake well to combine. Add the dressing to the potatoes along with the onion, bell pepper, and cornichons and gently combine the salad. The salad can be served at room temperature or chilled.

*Note:* The salad can be made up to 1 day in advance and refrigerated, tightly covered with plastic wrap.

Sweet potatoes make a wonderful cold salad, and they need very little adornment since their natural flavor is so extraordinary. The simple mustard vinaigrette provides a great flavor contrast, and the chopped pickles are an unexpected treat.

*Yams are the first food imported from the Americas by European explorers. Christopher Columbus writes about eating them on his first voyage, and they appear in England as early as the late 16th century.*

This colorful salad is the perfect summer side dish if you're serving any grilled entree with an Asian marinade. You can also add some leftover chicken or fish to the rice and serve it as an appetizer or lunch dish.

## Jasmine Rice Salad

[ Serves 6 to 8 ]

### Salad

1 1/2 cups jasmine rice

2 tablespoons vegetable oil

4 garlic cloves, minced

1 large shallot, peeled and minced

3 cups water

3/4 teaspoon salt

1 large carrot, peeled and shredded

1 red bell pepper, seeds and ribs removed, cut into a fine julienne

6 scallions, trimmed, cut into 1-inch sections, and cut into a fine julienne

### Dressing

1/2 cup rice wine vinegar

1/4 cup (firmly packed) dark brown sugar

2 tablespoons Thai or Vietnamese fish sauce

1 to 2 teaspoons chili sauce with garlic

1/4 cup vegetable oil

*1.* To prepare the rice, rinse the rice in a sieve under cold running water. Heat the oil in a large saucepan over medium heat. Add the garlic and shallots and sauté, stirring constantly, for 3 minutes, or until the shallots are translucent. Add the rice, water, and salt and cover the pan. Bring the rice to a boil over high heat. Reduce the heat to low and simmer the rice for 20 minutes, or until liquid is absorbed. Remove the pan from the heat. Allow the rice to rest, covered, for 10 minutes, then fluff it with a fork.

*2.* Prepare the dressing while the rice is cooking. Combine the vinegar, brown sugar, fish sauce, and chili sauce in a jar with a tight-fitting lid. Shake well until sugar is dissolved. Add the oil. Shake well again.

*3.* Place the rice in a mixing bowl or serving dish. Pour the dressing over the hot rice. Add the carrot, red pepper, and scallions. Mix well to combine. Refrigerate the salad until chilled, tightly covered with plastic wrap.

*Note:* The salad can be made up to 2 days in advance. Other vegetables that can be added are sliced raw celery or sliced cooked asparagus.

*An old Chinese New Year's greeting says "May your rice never burn," so we know that this is a common problem. The way to get rid of the burnt taste and save the rice is to scoop it out into a clean pot, leaving the burnt layer behind. Then cover the top of the rice with a layer of onion skins, and cover the pot for 10 minutes. Don't ask me why it works, but it does.*

Although a member of the onion family, leeks become very sweet when cooked slowly. When added to creamy potatoes, they also give the dish a pale green tone that's very elegant when served with roasted meats or poultry.

*Although we only cook with the white end of the leeks, don't discard the green tops. Use them for making stocks; they add a wonderful flavor and attractive dark color to the broths.*

# Leek and Potato Puree

[ Serves 6 ]

5 large Russet potatoes, peeled and cut into 1 1/2-inch pieces

4 cups finely chopped leeks, white parts only, rinsed and well drained

6 tablespoons unsalted butter

2 garlic cloves, minced

3/4 cup milk or half-and-half, heated

Salt and freshly ground pepper to taste

158

*1.* Put the potatoes in a saucepan and add cold water to cover. Salt the water and bring the potatoes to a boil over high heat. Boil the potatoes for 15 minutes, or until tender. Drain well.

*2.* While the potatoes are cooking bring another saucepan of water to a boil over high heat. Add the leeks, boil them for 5 minutes, and drain well. Melt the butter in a skillet over medium heat. Add the garlic and sauté for 3 minutes. Add the leeks and cook them over low heat, stirring frequently, for 10 minutes, or until the leeks are soft. Scrape the mixture into a food processor fitted with a steel blade, add the hot milk, and puree until smooth.

*3.* Put the potatoes through a food mill or ricer, or mash them by hand. Stir the leek mixture into the potatoes, and season with salt and freshly ground black pepper. Serve immediately.

*Note:* The dish can be prepared 6 hours in advance and kept at room temperature. Reheat it, covered, over low heat, stirring occasionally.

# Yams à la Churchill

[ Serves 6 ]

4 to 5 large yams or sweet potatoes
(about 12 ounces each)

3 navel oranges

2 lemons

3/4 cup (1 1/2 sticks) unsalted butter, melted

1 1/2 cups (firmly packed) dark brown sugar

1. Preheat the oven to 400° F.

2. Peel the yams and cut them into 1/2-inch slices. Peel the oranges and lemons, removing the bitter white pith. Thinly slice the oranges and lemons, discarding the lemon seeds. Combine the melted butter and sugar and set aside.

3. Place an overlapping layer of sweet potatoes in an ovenproof casserole or baking pan. Spread the layer with half of the butter mixture. Top the layer with half the orange and lemon slices. Repeat with another layer of potatoes, butter mixture, and fruit.

4. Cover the casserole with a lid or a sheet of heavy-duty aluminum foil. Bake for 45 minutes. Remove the cover, baste the yams with the juices from the pan, and bake, uncovered, for 15 to 25 minutes more, or until the yam slices can be easily pierced with a knife and the liquid has thickened into a glaze. Serve hot.

*Note:* The yams can be prepared 1 day in advance and reheated in a 350° F. oven, tightly covered with aluminum foil, for 15 to 20 minutes, or until hot.

This easy and spectacular recipe was passed along by Agnes Churchill to her daughter-in-law, Cecelia, and then to my friend Janet Churchill Morell. It's the best yam or sweet potato recipe I've ever tasted, since the sweetness of the brown sugar is balanced by the acidity in the citrus fruits.

*Yams have a higher moisture content than sweet potatoes, so if you're using sweet potatoes for this dish, you might want to add a few extra tablespoons of orange juice to the casserole.*

# All Dressed Up:
## Spreads, Sauces, Dips, & Dressings

This spread, based on one from Diane Worthington's *Cuisine of California*, takes but minutes to make, and its taste is exquisite. You can serve it from a bowl surrounded by crackers or toasts, or place it in a pastry bag and pipe it onto cucumber slices as a canapé.

*If smoked trout is not available, smoked whitefish or sturgeon are the best substitutes.*

*A pretty way to serve the spread is to line a small bowl or mold with plastic wrap and pack it with the trout spread. To serve, invert the mold onto a platter and decorate the mousse with chopped pickle.*

# Smoked Trout Spread

[ Makes 2 cups ]

1 cup sweet pickle slices, drained

1 pound smoked trout fillets, skinned and broken into 1-inch pieces

1/3 cup mayonnaise

1/4 cup heavy cream

1/4 cup freshly squeezed lemon juice

1/2 teaspoon cayenne

162

1. Place the pickle slices in a food processor fitted with a steel blade. Finely chop, pulsing. Scrape the chopped pickles into a mixing bowl, and set aside.
2. Place the trout, mayonnaise, cream, lemon juice, and cayenne in the workbowl of the food processor and puree until smooth. Scrape the trout mixture into the mixing bowl and stir well to combine. Refrigerate until well chilled.

*Note:* The spread can be made up to 2 days in advance and refrigerated, tightly covered.

# Two Salmon Spread

[ Makes 2 cups ]

1/2 pound salmon fillet

1 teaspoon Old Bay seasoning

1 pound cream cheese, softened

3 tablespoons freshly squeezed lemon juice

2 tablespoons white horseradish

1/4 pound smoked salmon, finely chopped

1/3 cup chopped scallion

3 tablespoons chopped fresh dill or
  2 teaspoons dried dill

Freshly ground black pepper to taste

1. Sprinkle the salmon fillet with the Old Bay seasoning and place it in a microwave-safe dish. Cover the dish with plastic wrap and microwave the fish on HIGH (100%) for 3 minutes, or until cooked through. Refrigerate the salmon until cold. Remove and discard the skin, and break the salmon into 1-inch chunks.

2. Place the salmon, cream cheese, lemon juice, and horseradish in a food processor fitted with a steel blade. Puree until smooth. Scrape the mixture into a mixing bowl and stir in the smoked salmon, scallion, and dill. Season with pepper and refrigerate until well chilled.

*Note:* The spread can be made 2 days in advance and refrigerated, tightly covered.

Delicate salmon is joined with succulent smoked salmon and seasonings in this easy to make spread. It is as at home on the brunch table as a topping for bagels as it is at a cocktail party. It has an attractive blushing pink color and an addictive flavor.

*For an easy canapé, pipe the spread onto toasted bread slices using the fluted tip of a pastry bag.*

163

This is a light and refreshing vegetable dip for the ubiquitous crudité platter. I keep it on hand at all times, since it also serves as a tasty dressing for egg or chicken salad.

*Crudité baskets are more for show than for sustenance, so don't go overboard on the quantity of vegetables unless you want to do a chopped salad the next day. The whole idea for the basket is color contrast and presentation. Here are the vegetables I serve raw: peeled baby carrots (preferably with a few inches of the green tops still attached), cucumber spears from seedless English cucumbers, thin strips of yellow and red pepper, and a assortment of cherry tomatoes. Other vegetables should really be blanched. They are sugar snap or snow peas, broccoli and cauliflower florets, green beans, and brussels sprouts.*

# Dill and Scallion Dip

[ Makes 2 cups ]

1 cup sour cream

3/4 cup mayonnaise

1/4 cup freshly squeezed lemon juice

1/3 cup finely chopped scallions

1/4 cup chopped fresh dill

3 garlic cloves, minced

Salt and freshly ground black pepper to taste

164

*1.* Whisk the sour cream, mayonnaise, and lemon juice together until smooth. Stir in the scallions, dill, and garlic. Season with salt and pepper and refrigerate until well chilled.

*Note:* The dip can be made up to 3 days in advance and refrigerated, tightly covered.

# Blue Cheese Dip

[ Makes 1 1/2 cups ]

3/4 cup mayonnaise

1/2 cup sour cream

2 tablespoons white wine vinegar

1/3 pound blue cheese, crumbled

Salt and freshly ground black pepper to taste

---

*1.* Whisk the mayonnaise, sour cream, and vinegar together until smooth. Stir in the blue cheese, season with salt and pepper, and refrigerate until well chilled.

*Note:* The dip can be made 3 days in advance and refrigerated, tightly covered.

After years of experimentation, I finally decided that a combination of mayonnaise and sour cream produced the best blue cheese dip. I hope you agree.

*This dip also makes a great topping for grilled steaks, or it can be thinned with some heavy cream and used as a salad dressing. For an easy hors d'oeuvre, place thin slices of grilled sirloin or tenderloin on crackers and top with a teaspoon of this dip.*

Heady with garlic and aromatic thyme, this easy spread is wonderful with crudités or on crackers with cocktails.

*While it's not totally fat-free, this bean spread is low in fat. Serve it in place of butter or olive oil with bread, the way they do in Italy.*

*Try this spread as an alternative to mayonnaise on various sandwiches. It's especially good with grilled chicken.*

## Tuscan White Bean Spread

[ Makes 4 cups ]

Two 15-ounce cans white cannellini beans
    or navy beans, drained and rinsed

1/3 cup extra virgin olive oil

1/4 cup freshly squeezed lemon juice

5 garlic cloves, peeled

1/2 cup Italian flat-leaf parsley leaves

1 tablespoon fresh thyme leaves or
    1 teaspoon dried thyme

2 roasted red bell peppers, peeled, seeded,
    and cut into 1-inch dice

Salt and freshly ground black pepper to taste

1. Combine the beans, olive oil, lemon juice, and garlic in a food processor fitted with a steel blade. Puree until smooth.

2. Add the parsley, thyme, and red peppers and finely chop, pulsing. Season with salt and pepper and chill well before serving.

*Note:* The spread can be made up to 4 days in advance and refrigerated, tightly covered.

# Sun-Dried Tomato Spread

[ Makes 3 cups ]

1/2 pound cream cheese, softened

1/2 cup mayonnaise

1/2 cup sour cream

3 garlic cloves, peeled

2 teaspoons herbes de provence

1/2 cup sun-dried tomatoes packed in oil, drained

4 scallions, trimmed and cut into 1-inch sections

Salt and freshly ground black pepper to taste

*1.* Combine the cream cheese, mayonnaise, sour cream, garlic, and herbes de provence in a food processor fitted with a steel blade. Puree until smooth. Add the sun-dried tomatoes and scallions to the workbowl and finely chop them, pulsing. Season with salt and pepper and refrigerate until well chilled.

*Note:* The spread can be prepared 3 days in advance and refrigerated, tightly covered.

This colorful and vibrantly flavored spread has myriad uses. I serve it with crackers as an hors d'oeuvre, as a sauce for grilled foods—ranging from meats and poultry to vegetables—and as a dressing for chicken salad.

*Save the oil that's drained off the sun-dried tomatoes. It's wonderful in salad dressings or for making homemade mayonnaise or aïoli.*

This easy spread has all the tantalizing flavors of traditional Southwestern food, and it's a snap to make since it uses canned beans.

*I use this spread to make all sorts of wrap sandwiches, as well as for topping tortilla chips and vegetable slices.*

## Black Bean Spread

[ Makes 4 cups ]

1/3 cup olive oil

1 onion, peeled and chopped

3 garlic cloves, minced

Two 15-ounce cans black beans, drained and rinsed

1/2 cup sour cream

1/4 cup freshly squeezed lime juice

1 teaspoon ground coriander

1 teaspoon ground cumin

1 tablespoon chopped fresh oregano or 1 teaspoon dried oregano

1 teaspoon Tabasco sauce, or to taste

1/2 cup chopped pimiento

1/4 cup chopped cilantro

Salt to taste

168

1. Heat the olive oil in a skillet over medium heat. Add the onion and garlic and sauté, stirring constantly, for 3 minutes, or until the onion is translucent. Scrape the mixture into a mixing bowl and set aside.
2. Combine the beans, sour cream, lime juice, coriander, cumin, oregano, and Tabasco in a food processor fitted with a steel blade. Puree until smooth and scrape the mixture into the mixing bowl with the vegetables. Stir in the pimiento and cilantro and season with salt. Refrigerate until well chilled.

*Note:* The spread can be made 4 days in advance and refrigerated, tightly covered.

# Summer Tomato Salsa

[ Makes 4 cups ]

5 large ripe tomatoes, cored, seeded, and chopped

1/2 red onion, peeled and finely chopped

1/2 red bell pepper, seeds and ribs removed, finely chopped

1 or 2 small fresh serrano or jalapeño chilies, seeds and ribs removed, finely chopped

4 garlic cloves, minced

3 tablespoons chopped cilantro

1 tablespoon chopped fresh oregano or 1 teaspoon dried oregano

1 tablespoon chopped fresh basil or 1/2 teaspoon dried basil

1/4 cup red wine vinegar

2 tablespoons olive oil

Salt and freshly ground black pepper to taste

*1.* Combine all the ingredients in a glass or stainless steel bowl. Stir gently and refrigerate for at least 1 hour to blend the flavors.

*Note:* The salsa can be prepared up to 2 days in advance and refrigerated, tightly covered.

One bite of this salsa and I'm emotionally transported to a Mexican beach, sipping margaritas and using crispy wedges of tortillas to scoop the salsa. You can make it as mild or spicy as you want by cutting back or increasing the number of hot chilies.

*I use this salsa as a topping for grilled foods such as chicken breasts or pork chops.*

*Generally, the smaller the chili pepper the hotter it is. That's why this recipe calls for the same number of tiny serrano chilies as larger jalapeños.*

This is my "house dressing," and I keep a batch of it ready to go at all times. Like all salad dressings, it's incredibly easy to make, and the difference between homemade and bottled dressings is enormous.

*This dressing makes an excellent marinade for meat, poultry, or seafood. Combine equal parts of dressing and wine in a heavy plastic bag and marinate foods for 30 minutes before grilling or broiling.*

*In addition to tossed salads, try this as the dressing for a cold pasta salad.*

# Balsamic Vinaigrette

[ Makes 1 1/2 cups ]

2 shallots, peeled and finely chopped

5 garlic cloves, minced

1/3 cup balsamic vinegar

3 tablespoons sherry vinegar

3 tablespoons Dijon mustard

1 tablespoon chopped parsley

2 teaspoons herbes de provence

Salt and freshly ground black pepper to taste

3/4 cup extra virgin olive oil

170

1. Combine the shallots, garlic, balsamic vinegar, sherry vinegar, mustard, parsley, herbes de provence, and salt and pepper in a jar with a tight-fitting lid. Shake well. Add the olive oil and shake well again. Refrigerate until well chilled.

*Note:* The dressing can be made up to 4 days in advance and refrigerated, tightly covered.

# Ginger Vinaigrette

[ Makes 1 1/2 cups ]

2 tablespoons sesame seeds

1/2 cup rice wine vinegar

1/4 cup freshly squeezed lime juice

2 tablespoons soy sauce

3 shallots, peeled and minced

3 garlic cloves, minced

2 tablespoons grated ginger

1 tablespoon chopped cilantro

3 tablespoons sesame oil

2/3 cup vegetable oil

Salt and freshly ground black pepper to taste

*1.* Place the sesame seeds in a small dry skillet over medium heat. Toast the seeds, stirring constantly, for 2 minutes, or until lightly brown. Remove the skillet from the heat and set aside.
*2.* Combine the sesame seeds, vinegar, lime juice, soy sauce, shallots, garlic, ginger, and cilantro in a jar with a tight-fitting lid. Shake well. Add the sesame oil and vegetable oil and shake well again. Season with salt and pepper and refrigerate until well chilled.

*Note:* The dressing can be made up to 4 days in advance and refrigerated, tightly covered.

*I* make a lot of Asian-inspired food, and this salad dressing made with mild rice vinegar complements those dishes well, since it contains characteristic Asian seasoning and sesame oil.

*This dressing is perfect for a cold stir-fried vegetable salad made with ingredients such as bok choy and broccoli. I also use it to turn leftover cold rice into a salad.*

171

This dressing is extremely luxurious, if for no other reason than the high cost of hazelnut oil. But it's worth every penny. The crunchy toasted hazelnuts combined with the hazelnut oil produce a dressing with interesting texture and delightful aroma and flavor.

*In addition to tossing this dressing with green salads, I also use it as a simple sauce for grilled chicken breasts and any sort of seafood.*

# Hazelnut Vinaigrette

[ Makes 2 cups ]

1 cup hazelnuts

3 tablespoons sherry vinegar

3 tablespoons Madeira

1 tablespoon Dijon mustard

1 teaspoon sugar

Salt and freshly ground black pepper to taste

1 cup hazelnut oil

*1.* Preheat the oven to 350°F.

*2.* Place the hazelnuts on a baking sheet and toast them for 8 to 10 minutes, or until they are lightly browned. Let cool and transfer them to a food processor fitted with the steel blade. Finely chop them, pulsing. Set aside.

*3.* Combine the vinegar, Madeira, mustard, sugar, and salt and pepper in a jar with a tight-fitting lid. Shake well. Add the hazelnut oil and hazelnuts and shake well again. Refrigerate until well chilled.

*Note:* The dressing can be made up to 4 days in advance and refrigerated, tightly covered.

# My Favorite Barbecue Sauce

[ Makes 4 cups ]

One 20-ounce bottle ketchup

1 cup cider vinegar

1/2 cup (firmly packed) dark brown sugar

5 tablespoons Worcestershire sauce

1/4 cup vegetable oil

2 tablespoons dry mustard

2 garlic cloves, minced

1 tablespoon grated fresh ginger

1 lemon, thinly sliced

1/2 to 1 teaspoon Tabasco sauce, to taste

*1.* Combine all the ingredients in a saucepan and bring to a boil over medium heat, stirring occasionally. Reduce the heat to low and simmer the sauce, uncovered, for 30 minutes, or until thick, stirring occasionally. Strain the sauce, pressing with the back of a spoon to extract as much liquid as possible. Ladle the sauce into containers and refrigerate, tightly covered.

*Note:* The sauce can be made 1 week in advance and refrigerated, tightly covered.

*There are hundreds of variations on American barbecue sauce; mine includes some lemon and ginger to add complex nuances to the basic tomato flavor.*

*When basting foods on the grill with this or any other barbecue sauce, baste for only the last few minutes of grilling since the sugar will burn and char the foods.*

*Our word barbecue, which appears in American dictionaries before the Revolutionary War, comes from the Spanish* **barbacoa**, *which refers to the framework of sticks over which food was cooked.*

Sweet-and-sour sauces play a role in all Asian cuisines and this one is zesty, and has tangy pineapple juice as its base.

*I serve this as a dipping sauce for Asian hors d'oeuvres such as potstickers, and it's also a great grilling sauce for any meat, fish, or poultry.*

# Indonesian Barbecue Sauce

[ Makes 4 cups ]

3 cups pineapple juice

1 1/2 cups distilled white vinegar

3/4 cup soy sauce

1/4 cup finely chopped fresh ginger

1 1/2 cups ketchup

3/4 cup (firmly packed) dark brown sugar

1/2 cup chopped cilantro

3/4 cup freshly squeezed lime juice

*174*

1. Combine the pineapple juice, vinegar, soy sauce, and ginger in a saucepan. Bring to a boil over medium heat and boil until the liquid is reduced by half, stirring occasionally. Add the ketchup and brown sugar to the pan, reduce the heat to low, and simmer the sauce for 5 minutes.

2. Remove the pan from the heat and stir in the cilantro and lime juice. Ladle the sauce into containers and refrigerate until well chilled.

*Note:* The sauce can be made 5 days in advance and refrigerated, tightly covered.

# Spicy Thai Peanut Sauce

[ Makes 4 cups ]

1 cup chunky peanut butter

1/2 cup hot water

1/2 cup (firmly packed) dark brown sugar

1/3 cup freshly squeezed lime juice

1/4 cup soy sauce

2 tablespoons Asian sesame oil

2 tablespoons Asian chili paste

6 garlic cloves, minced

3 scallions, trimmed and chopped

1/4 cup chopped cilantro

*1.* Combine the peanut butter, water, brown sugar, lime juice, soy sauce, sesame oil, and chili paste in a mixing bowl. Whisk until well combined. Stir in the garlic, scallions, and cilantro and chill well before serving.

*Note:* The sauce can be prepared 5 days in advance and refrigerated, tightly covered.

*There* are many ways to make peanut sauce, some of them cooked and some not. I take the easy way out and use commercial peanut butter as the base, so this rich and luscious sauce can be created in a matter of minutes.

*Here are some of the ways I use this versatile sauce: as a dipping sauce for any grilled satay, tossed with cold pasta and strips of vegetables such as red bell pepper and steamed snow peas for an Asian pasta salad, or as a dressing for chicken, turkey, or shrimp salad.*

*Larger limes that are shaped like lemons tend to be sweeter than small limes.*

Vegetables absorb the flavor from aromatic woods as do meats and seafood. This chutney is a wonderful condiment for any grilled, baked, or broiled meats. For an instant hors d'oeuvre, use the chutney to top a block of cream cheese.

*Chutney is a traditional Indian condiment that made its way into English cooking by the 17th century.*

*Use a few tablespoons of this chutney and an equal amount of wine to deglaze the pan after sautéing chicken breasts or pork chops.*

## Smoked Apple Chutney

[ Makes 4 cups ]

1 cup hickory or applewood chips

6 large tomatoes, cut in half

1 large onion, cut in half

4 garlic cloves, peeled

2 apples, peeled, cored, and quartered

1 cup sugar

3/4 cup cider vinegar

1/4 cup golden raisins

1/4 cup dried currants

2 tablespoons grated fresh ginger

1/2 teaspoon cayenne

Salt to taste

*1.* Light a charcoal or gas grill. Soak the wood chips in cold water for 30 minutes. Drain the wood chips and place them on the fire.

*2.* Cover the grill with a small-holed fish grill and place the tomatoes, onion, garlic, and apples on the grill. Cover the grill with a lid and smoke the vegetables and apples for 10 minutes.

*3.* Remove the vegetables and apples from the grill. Peel, core, and seed the tomatoes. Peel and finely dice the onion, garlic, and apples. Place them in a large saucepan and add the sugar, vinegar, raisins, currants, ginger, and cayenne.

*4.* Bring the chutney to a boil over medium heat. Simmer, uncovered, for 30 minutes, or until thick, stirring occasionally. Season with salt to taste. Ladle the chutney into containers and refrigerate.

*Note:* The chutney can be made 5 days in advance and refrigerated, tightly covered.

# Cranberry Chutney

[ Makes 4 cups ]

1 pound fresh cranberries

1 cup water

1 3/4 cups sugar

1 cup golden raisins

3/4 cup red wine vinegar

1/2 cup red wine

2 tablespoons molasses

2 tablespoons grated fresh ginger

1 tablespoon curry powder

1 tablespoon Worcestershire sauce

1/2 to 1 teaspoon Tabasco sauce, to taste

1. Rinse the cranberries, picking out any shriveled ones or twigs. Combine the cranberries with the water and sugar in a large saucepan and bring to a boil over medium heat, stirring occasionally. Boil for 10 minutes, or until the cranberries pop.

2. Add the raisins, vinegar, wine, molasses, ginger, curry, Worcestershire sauce, and Tabasco. Reduce the heat to low and simmer the chutney, uncovered, for 20 minutes, or until thickened. Ladle the chutney into containers and refrigerate, tightly covered.

Note: The chutney keeps well for up to 1 month, refrigerated tightly covered.

I serve this vivid chutney at Thanksgiving dinner and also as an accompaniment to any grilled or smoked meat—from pork roast to venison. Its sweet-hot seasoning creates a far more complex flavor than a traditional cranberry sauce.

There is perhaps no food more closely associated with New England's tribes of Native Americans than the cranberry. They pounded them with animal fat to produce pemmican, which they then dried and ate for protein. They often sweetened cranberries with maple sugar, and they used their vivid hue as a dye. The name cranberry was developed centuries later by the Dutch. It comes from the word **kraanbere**, which is Low German.

# Grand Finales:
## Cakes, Pies, & Cookies

The perky flavor of Asian crystallized ginger fills every bite of this simple, homey cake made with molasses—a New England staple. The cream cheese frosting is the perfect, creamy accent.

# Ginger Cake

[ Serves 8 to 10 ]

### Ginger Cake

2 1/2 cups all-purpose flour

2 teaspoons ground ginger

1 teaspoon baking soda

1/2 teaspoon salt

3/4 cup (1 1/2 sticks) unsalted butter, softened

1 cup granulated sugar

1 large egg, lightly beaten

2 tablespoons finely chopped crystallized ginger

1/2 cup unsulfured molasses

1 cup buttermilk

### Cream Cheese Frosting

6 cups (1 1/2 pounds) confectioners' sugar

Three 8-ounce packages cream cheese, softened

6 tablespoons (3/4 stick) unsalted butter, softened

2 teaspoons vanilla extract

### Crunch Topping

8 to 10 gingersnap cookies

1 cup chopped pecans, toasted in a 350°F. oven for 5 minutes

*1.* Preheat the oven to 350°F. Grease and flour two 8-inch round cake pans.

*2.* To make the cake, combine the flour, ground ginger, baking soda, and salt and set aside. Cream the butter and sugar in a large mixing bowl with an electric mixer at medium-high speed until light and fluffy. Add the egg, crystallized ginger, and molasses and beat well. Add the dry ingredients and buttermilk alternately and beat at low speed until smooth. Divide the batter between the prepared pans and bake for 35 minutes, or until a cake tester or toothpick inserted in center of each layer comes out clean. Immediately invert the cake layers onto cooling racks and cool completely.

*3.* To make the frosting, combine all the frosting ingredients in a mixing bowl. Start an electric mixer at low speed to combine, then beat at high speed for 2 minutes, or until light and fluffy.

*4.* To make the crunch topping, break the gingersnaps into pieces, and finely chop them in a food processor fitted with a steel blade, pulsing; you should have 1/2 cup of crumbs. Combine the crumbs with the pecans and set aside.

*5.* To assemble the cake, place overlapping sheets of wax paper on a cake plate. Split the cake layers horizontally into 2 halves. Place 1 layer, top side down, on the paper and spread with 1/2 cup of the frosting. Place a second layer on top of it and spread with 1/2 cup frosting. Top with the other 2 layers with frosting in between them. Spread the remaining frosting on the top and sides of the cake. Chill the cake for at least 2 hours, or until the frosting has set. Pat the crunch mixture on the sides of the cake and sprinkle it on top.

*Note:* The cake can be made up to 1 day in advance and refrigerated, loosely covered with plastic wrap. Allow it to sit out for at least 2 hours before serving.

*It was the custom during Nantucket's whaling era for wives to scan the horizon in hope they would sight their husband's returning ship. When that occurred, they would make a large batch of gingerbread cake as a celebration.*

Jodi Levesque is one of the most talented pastry chefs I know, and I'm honored to have her sinfully rich and moist carrot cake in this book. The addition of pineapple and coconut to the batter adds additional textures, flavors, and moisture.

*While we think of carrot cake as the epitome of the homey American cake, it is a relative newcomer. Food historian Evan Jones traces it back only to the early 1960s, as the winner of the baking contest at the Guadalupe County Fair in Seguin, Texas. With the rise of vegetarianism during the same decade, many cooks began exploring the potential of vegetables such as inherently sweet carrots and moist zucchini for dessert recipes.*

# Jodi Levesque's Carrot Cake
[ Serves 10 to 12 ]

2 cups all-purpose flour

1 tablespoon cinnamon

2 teaspoons baking soda

1/2 teaspoon salt

1 1/2 cups vegetable oil

1 1/2 cups sugar

4 eggs, at room temperature

1 1/2 teaspoons vanilla extract

1 pound carrots, peeled and shredded

1/2 cup sweetened coconut

1/2 cup crushed pineapple packed in juice, drained

1/2 cup chopped walnuts, toasted in a 350°F. oven for 5 minutes

1 batch Cream Cheese Frosting (page 180)

*1.* Preheat the oven to 350°F. Grease and flour three 9-inch round cake pans with 1 1/2-inch sides.

*2.* Sift the flour with the cinnamon, baking soda, and salt and set aside. Place the vegetable oil, sugar, eggs, and vanilla in a mixing bowl and beat at medium speed with an electric mixer until well blended. Add the dry ingredients and beat at low speed until just blended in. Stir in the carrots, coconut, pineapple, and walnuts.

*3.* Divide the batter among the prepared pans and bake for 35 to 40 minutes, or until the cake begins to shrink away from the sides of the pan and a cake tester inserted in the center of each layer comes out clean. Cool the cake layers on a rack for 15 minutes, then invert the layers onto racks and allow them to cool completely.

*4.* Prepare the frosting. Place 2 overlapping sheets of wax paper on a platter. Place 1 layer, flat side down, on the paper and spread with 3/4 cup of the frosting. Repeat with the second layer. Top with the third layer and spread the remaining frosting on the top and sides. Refrigerate the cake for at least 2 hours before serving.

*Note:* The layers can be prepared 3 days in advance and refrigerated, tightly covered. The cake can be assembled 1 day in advance and refrigerated.

# Cranberry Cake

[ Serves 10 to 12 ]

Cranberry Cake

3 cups cake flour

1 1/2 teaspoons baking soda

1/2 teaspoon salt

1-1/2 cups granulated sugar

1/2 cup (1 stick) unsalted butter, melted
   and cooled

2 large eggs

1 teaspoon grated orange zest

1 1/4 cups buttermilk

1 1/2 cups fresh cranberries

1 cup dried cranberries

Icing

4 tablespoons (1/2 stick) unsalted butter, melted

1 tablespoon freshly squeezed orange juice

1 teaspoon grated orange zest

1/2 cup confectioners' sugar

1. Preheat the oven to 350°F. Butter and flour a 10-inch bundt pan.
2. Sift the flour, baking soda, and salt together. Whisk the sugar, butter, eggs, and orange zest together in a large bowl. Whisk in one third of the flour mixture, then one third of the buttermilk. Repeat twice more, until all the ingredients are incorporated. Stir in the fresh cranberries and dried cranberries and scrape the batter into the prepared pan.
3. Bake the cake for 50 minutes, or until a toothpick inserted in the center comes out clean. Allow the cake to cool on a rack for 10 minutes, then invert it onto the rack to cool completely.
4. To prepare the icing, combine all the icing ingredients in a small bowl and stir well. Drizzle the icing over the cooled cake.

*Note:* The cake can be prepared 1 day in advance and kept covered at room temperature.

I'm infatuated with the tart flavor of cranberries, and I have made it a mission to devise recipes beyond variations on sauce. This cake has a double dose since it combines tart fresh cranberries with sweet dried cranberries. It's excellent at brunch or any time of day.

Early colonist William Byrd wrote in his 1711 diary that he "said my prayers and ate some cranberry tart for breakfast."

While other seasonal crops have been commercially frozen for years, the cranberry has not been part of that list. But it's very possible to freeze them yourself in heavy plastic bags for uses such as sauces or this cake.

This recipe is inspired by a similar dessert I enjoyed many times at cookbook author Sarah Leah Chase's table when we were neighbors in Tom Nevers, the section of the island where I live. The chocolate ganache center remains liquid after the cakes are baked, and they are a very elegant ending for a special dinner.

*Like fine wine, dark chocolate actually improves with age. Store it tightly wrapped in a cool place. Even if the chocolate has developed a gray "bloom" from being stored at too high a temperature, it is still fine to use for cooking.*

# Warm Chocolate Tortes

[ Serves 6 ]

5 ounces bittersweet chocolate, chopped and divided

2 tablespoons heavy cream

1 tablespoon rum or fruit-flavored liqueur

5 tablespoons unsalted butter

2 eggs

1 egg yolk

1/4 cup sugar

1/4 cup all-purpose flour

Whipped cream or ice cream, for serving

184

*1.* Grease 6 muffin tins. Melt 2 ounces of the chocolate with the cream and rum in a small microwave-safe dish. Stir well and refrigerate to harden. Form the chocolate into 6 balls and refrigerate until ready to use.

*2.* Preheat the oven to 350°F.

*3.* Melt the remaining chocolate with the butter and allow to cool. Place the eggs, egg yolk, and sugar in a medium mixing bowl. Beat with an electric mixer at medium and then high speed until very thick and triple in volume. Fold the cooled chocolate into the eggs, then fold in the flour.

*4.* Divide the batter among the muffin tins and push a chocolate ball into the center of each tin. Bake the tortes for 10 to 12 minutes, or until the sides are set. Remove the pan from the oven and invert onto a baking sheet. Serve immediately, with whipped cream or ice cream.

*Note:* The tortes can be prepared up to 2 hours before baking them.

# Flourless Chocolate Nut Torte

[ Serves 6 ]

10 ounces bittersweet chocolate, chopped

2 cups pecan or walnut halves, toasted in a 350° F. oven for 5 minutes

2 tablespoons plus 1/2 cup sugar

1 cup (2 sticks) unsalted butter, softened

3 large eggs, room temperature

1 tablespoon rum

1. Preheat the oven to 375°F. Grease an 8-inch round cake pan, cut out a circle of wax paper or parchment to fit the bottom, and grease the paper.

2. Melt 4 ounces of the chocolate in a microwave oven or over simmering water in a double boiler. Cool slightly. Reserve 12 nut halves and chop the remaining nuts with the 2 tablespoons of sugar in a food processor fitted with a steel blade, pulsing. Scrape the nuts into a bowl. Beat 1/2 cup (1 stick) of the butter and the remaining 1/2 cup sugar in the processor until light and fluffy. Add the melted chocolate, then add the eggs, one at a time. Beat well between each addition and scrape the sides of the workbowl with a rubber spatula. Add the rum, then fold the chocolate mixture into the ground nuts.

3. Scrape the batter into the prepared pan and bake the cake for 25 minutes. The cake will be soft but will firm up as it cools. Remove the cake from the oven and cool 20 minutes on a rack. Invert the cake onto a plate, remove the paper, and cool completely.

4. To make a glaze, combine the remaining 6 ounces of chocolate and remaining 1/2 cup (1 stick) of butter in a small saucepan. Melt over low heat and beat until shiny and smooth. Place the cake on a rack over a sheet of wax paper. Pour the glaze onto the center of the cake, and rotate the rack at an angle so the glaze runs down the sides. Top with the nut halves, and allow to sit in a cool place until the chocolate has hardened.

*Note:* The cake can be prepared 1 day in advance and refrigerated. Allow it to reach room temperature before serving.

The batter for this luscious chocolate cake is created in a matter of minutes in a food processor. It's a dense and rich cake that is crunchy with nuts and topped with a candy-like ganache.

*If you find that the parchment paper sticks to the bottom of the cake, brush the paper with a little warm water. After ten seconds the paper will peel right off.*

I associate this dessert with Memorial Day on Nantucket, which is when our strawberry crop is likely to be at its peak. The lemony, creamy filling for this pie is a traditional English curd. It's the perfect foil for strawberries, or you can use other berries when they're in season.

*An easy way to collect tiny bits of citrus zest is to cover the small side of your grater with a sheet of parchment paper. Rub the lemon over the grater and the bits will remain on the paper.*

*If you want to serve this as part of a display of miniature pastries, the recipe makes enough to fill two dozen miniature phyllo cups, manufactured by Athens and found in the freezer section of the supermarket.*

## Lemon and Strawberry Tart

[ Serves 6 to 8 ]

5 egg yolks

1/2 cup sugar

1/4 cup freshly squeezed lemon juice

1 tablespoon grated lemon zest

6 tablespoons (3/4 stick) unsalted butter, cut into small pieces

One 9-inch prebaked pie shell

2 quarts strawberries, stemmed and sliced

1/2 cup beach plum or red currant jelly, melted

1. Whisk the egg yolks and sugar in a small saucepan for 2 minutes, or until thick and lemon colored. Add the lemon juice and lemon zest and whisk again well. Place the saucepan over low heat and cook, stirring constantly, until warm and slightly thickened. Do not let the mixture come to a boil or the egg yolks will scramble.

2. Remove the pan from the heat and add the butter. Whisk until smooth, then refrigerate the curd with a sheet of plastic wrap pressed directly onto the surface.

3. Spread the curd in the prebaked pie shell and top with the strawberries. Brush the berries with the melted jelly and serve as soon as possible.

*Note:* The curd can be prepared 2 days in advance and refrigerated, tightly covered. Do not assemble the tart more than a few hours before serving.

# Rhubarb Crumb Cake

[ Serves 6 to 8 ]

1 1/2 pounds rhubarb stalks

1/4 cup freshly squeezed orange juice

3 tablespoons plus 1/2 cup all-purpose flour

1 1/2 cups sugar

4 tablespoons (1/2 stick) unsalted butter

1/2 cup uncooked oatmeal (not instant)

One 9-inch pie shell, unbaked

1. Preheat the oven to 350°F.

2. Dice the rhubarb into 1-inch pieces and combine with the orange juice in a saucepan. Bring to a boil, reduce the heat, and simmer 2 minutes. Stir in 3 tablespoons of the flour and 1 cup of the sugar. Simmer for 7 minutes, stirring occasionally, until the rhubarb is barely tender.

3. While the rhubarb is simmering, combine the remaining 1/2 cup flour, 1/2 cup sugar, butter, and oatmeal in a mixing bowl. Blend the ingredients together with your fingertips until it resembles coarse crumbs.

4. Scrape the rhubarb into the pie shell and sprinkle with the crumb topping. Bake for 45 minutes, or until the crust is browned. Serve warm.

*Note:* The rhubarb mixture and topping can be prepared 1 day in advance and refrigerated, tightly covered. Do not bake the pie until the day it is to be served.

Fresh, bright red stalks of rhubarb are another harbinger of spring. While it is frequently paired with strawberries, I'm a purist and like the flavor of this "pie vegetable" by itself, perhaps topped with some strawberry ice cream.

*Rhubarb is Asian in origin, although it arrived in Europe in time to appear in the writings of both Pliny and Dioscorides. Its medicinal qualities were touted by European monks since the Middle Ages. The first recipes for rhubarb pie don't appear in cookbooks until the mid-19th century, and the vegetable was very popular with the Pennsylvania Dutch.*

*Rhubarb has huge, notched leaves, and I've seen many gardens on Nantucket that include it as a border plant. It is certainly "deer proof," since the leaves are poisonous to all species.*

There could be no more luscious blueberry pie than this one. The crème fraîche is the perfect backdrop for the innate sweetness of blueberries, and it's visually stunning.

*While Maine is most closely associated with succulent wild blueberries, they are present on Nantucket. Just as fishermen never divulge the best spots for casting a lure, so islanders carefully guard the locations of reliable bushes. Low-bush berries are found in the moors, and they are difficult to harvest. On the other hand, high-bush berries are easy to spot in the wetlands surrounding many of the island's ponds.*

# Blueberry Crème Fraîche Tart
[ Serves 6 to 8 ]

3 eggs

1/2 cup sugar

1 teaspoon vanilla extract

1-1/4 cups crème fraîche

1 pint fresh blueberries, rinsed

One 9-inch prebaked pie shell

1. Preheat the oven to 350°F.
2. Whisk the eggs and sugar in the top of a double boiler for 2 minutes, or until thick and lemon colored. Add the vanilla and crème fraîche and stir well. Place the mixture over water that is simmering in the bottom of the double boiler. Heat, stirring constantly, until the mixture is hot and starting to thicken.
3. Place the blueberries in the bottom of the pie shell and pour the warm custard over them. Bake for 10 minutes, or until the custard is set. Chill well before serving.

*Note:* The pie can be baked up to 1 day in advance.

# Crème Brulée Tart

[ Serves 6 ]

2 teaspoons unsalted butter

2 1/2 cups heavy cream

1 teaspoon vanilla extract

6 egg yolks

1/2 cup sugar

1/4 pound frozen puff pastry, defrosted

1/2 cup (firmly packed) dark brown sugar

*1.* Preheat the oven to 375°F. Grease a 6-cup soufflé dish with the butter, and set aside.

*2.* Bring the cream and vanilla to a boil over low heat in a heavy saucepan. While the cream is heating, beat the egg yolks and sugar in a mixing bowl until thick and lemon colored. Slowly add the hot cream, and pour the mixture into the prepared dish. Place the dish in a baking pan and pour boiling water halfway up the sides of the pan. Bake the custard for 30 to 40 minutes, or until the top is brown and a knife inserted in the center comes out clean. Remove the custard from the water bath and allow to cool.

*3.* While the custard is baking, roll the puff pastry into a 10-inch circle. Fit the pastry into a 9-inch false bottom tart pan. Press it into the sides and bottom of the pan, and bake the crust for 30 minutes, or until golden brown.

*4.* To finish the tart, preheat the oven broiler. Unmold the custard into the tart shell, and smooth it evenly to the sides with a spatula. Sift the brown sugar evenly over the top of the custard. Broil the tart 6 inches from the heat element for 2 minutes, or until the sugar is bubbling. Remove the tart from the oven and carefully remove it from the pan. Serve immediately.

*Note:* The pastry shell and custard can both be made 1 day in advance. Wrap the pastry with plastic wrap and keep it at room temperature. Refrigerate the custard, tightly wrapped. Allow the custard to reach room temperature before the final assembly and broiling.

Crème brulée is a treat in any season, and I usually serve this pie during the winter when there are few ripe fruits available. The light puff pastry crust makes the pie like a cream-topped cookie.

*While crème brulée—literally burnt cream—has a French name, it's most likely that the dish originated in England. British food authority Jane Grigson has said that recipes for it appeared in the early 17th century, so it is likely that the early New England settlers were aware of it.*

This pie—joining tart cranberries and juicy apples—is emblematic of fall in New England. It is always part of my Thanksgiving dessert table, and I serve it all during the winter.

*Cranberries are indigenous to North America, and they were shipped to London in the early 18th century, where they were marketed as "Cape Cod Bell Cranberries" and fetched a hefty price. The cranberry never gained much favor on the Continent except in Germany, since it is similar to a tart berry grown in northern parts of that country.*

*It's faster to slice apples if you just peel them and then start cutting slices off as you rotate the fruit. When you reach the core, toss it away.*

# Cranberry Apple Pie

[ Serves 6 to 8 ]

Enough pie crust for a 9-inch double-crust pie

2 cups fresh cranberries, rinsed

1/2 cup dried currants

4 Granny Smith apples, peeled, cored, and thinly sliced

1 cup sugar

3 tablespoons all-purpose flour

1/2 teaspoon cinnamon

3 tablespoons unsalted butter, cut into small pieces

190

*1.* Preheat the oven to 425°F.

*2.* Line a 9-inch pie plate with half the pastry. Combine the cranberries, currants, and apples in a large mixing bowl. Sprinkle with the sugar, flour, and cinnamon and toss to mix well.

*3.* Pile the filling into the crust, and arrange the butter on top. Roll out the second half of the crust, place it over the filling, seal, and flute the edges. Cut 4 slits in the top crust as steam vents.

*4.* Bake the pie for 15 minutes, then reduce the heat to 350°F. and continue to bake for 45 minutes more, or until the crust is brown. Serve warm or at room temperature.

*Note:* The pie can be made 1 day in advance and kept at room temperature.

# Chocolate Caramel Pecan Pie

[ Serves 6 to 8 ]

1 1/2 cups sugar

1/3 cup water

1 cup heavy cream

4 tablespoons (1/2 stick) unsalted butter, cut into small pieces

1/4 cup rum

2 eggs

1 cup pecan halves, toasted at 350°F. for 5 minutes

4 ounces bittersweet chocolate, melted

One 9-inch prebaked pie shell

*1.* Combine the sugar and water in a small saucepan and place over medium-high heat. Cook, without stirring, until the liquid is golden brown and caramelized. Turn off the heat and add the cream slowly, stirring with a long-handled spoon; it will bubble up at first. Once the cream has been added, cook the caramel over low heat for 2 minutes. Strain the mixture into a mixing bowl and allow it to cool for 10 minutes.

*2.* Preheat the oven to 400°F.

*3.* Beat the butter, rum, and eggs into the caramel and whisk until smooth. Stir in the pecans. Spread the melted chocolate in the bottom of the prebaked pie shell and pour the pecan filling over it. Bake for 15 minutes, then reduce the oven heat to 350°F. and bake for 15 minutes more. Serve the pie at room temperature.

*Note:* The pie can be made 1 day in advance and refrigerated, tightly covered. Bring it to room temperature before serving.

*I* believe that the first responsibility of any dessert is to contain at least some chocolate, and this pie is almost like eating a candy bar. It combines chocolate with crunchy pecans and mellow caramel.

*Caramelizing sugar is not difficult, but one pitfall is allowing the sugar to actually reach dark brown before removing the pan from the heat. The liquid and pot are very hot by the time the sugar starts to color, so take the pan off the heat when the syrup is a medium brown; it will continue to cook.*

Here's a dessert that children (as well as adults) all adore, and it's great in all seasons. The rich ganache and creamy peanut butter mousse are like a Reese's cup on your plate.

*Peanut butter is an American invention; it was introduced at the St. Louis World's Fair in 1904 as a health food.*

# Peanut Butter Mousse Pie

[ Serves 8 to 10 ]

1 cup creamy peanut butter

3/4 cup sugar

One 8-ounce package cream cheese, softened

1 tablespoon butter, melted

1 teaspoon vanilla extract

1 3/4 cups heavy cream

8 ounces bittersweet chocolate

One 9-inch chocolate cookie or graham cracker crumb crust

*192*

1. Beat the peanut butter and sugar with an electric mixer on medium speed until light and fluffy. Add the cream cheese, butter, and vanilla and beat well. In another mixing bowl, whip 3/4 cup of the cream until medium-soft peaks form and fold it into the peanut butter mixture until thoroughly combined. Refrigerate 30 minutes, or until slightly firm.

2. While the mousse is chilling, chop the chocolate into small pieces and place it in a mixing bowl. Bring the remaining 1 cup of cream to a boil over low heat in a small saucepan and pour it over the chocolate. Stir until melted and thoroughly combined. Pour the chocolate into the pie shell, reserving about 1/3 cup at room temperature. Chill until firmly set.

3. Remove the mousse from the refrigerator. Beat with an electric mixer on low speed for at least 5 minutes, preferably longer, until the mousse is light and fluffy. Cover the chocolate layer with the peanut butter mousse and distribute it evenly with a spatula. Place the remaining chocolate in a pastry bag fitted with the small tip or in a plastic bag with small hole at one corner. Drizzle it decoratively over the mousse. Chill until ready to serve.

*Note:* The pie can be prepared 1 day in advance, and refrigerated.

# Fresh Berries with Lemon Mousse

[ Serves 6 ]

6 egg yolks

3/4 cup sugar

1/2 cup freshly squeezed lemon juice

2 teaspoons grated lemon zest

2 tablespoons Grand Marnier

1 1/2 cups heavy cream

4 cups assorted fresh berries, such as blueberries, raspberries, blackberries, or sliced strawberries

*1.* Beat the egg yolks with the sugar in a saucepan until thick and light colored. Beat in the lemon juice and lemon zest and place the pan over low heat. Heat, stirring constantly, until the mixture is thick enough to coat the back of the spoon. Remove from the heat, beat in the Grand Marnier, and chill until cold.

*2.* Chill a mixing bowl and electric mixer beaters in the freezer. Beat the cream until stiff peaks form, then fold the whipped cream into the custard mixture. Chill for up to 3 hours before serving. To serve, divide the berries into dishes and spoon the mousse on top of them.

*Note:* The custard can be made up to 1 day in advance and refrigerated, tightly covered with plastic wrap. Do not whip the cream and fold the mixture longer than 3 hours in advance, or the mixture can separate.

One of the rites of spring on Nantucket is to trek the fields of Bartlett's Farm to pick your own strawberries. While fresh berries need little augmentation, I like to top them with this light mousse.

*The easiest way to get the most juice out of lemons is to have the fruit at room temperature and roll it around on a counter a few times before cutting it in half. If you need just a few tablespoons of lemon juice, squeeze the juice through the fingers of your other hand. That way you can catch and discard the seeds.*

These are dense, rich brownies, with a swirl of white cream cheese in the chocolate. For a change of pace, you can add some grated orange zest to the cream cheese mixture.

*Butter should be softened to beat properly with sugar for all batters and doughs. A fast way to soften it is to grate it through the large holes on a box grater. Do not soften it in the microwave; it will become too soft.*

## Marble Fudge Brownies

[ Makes 12 ]

1/2 cup (1 stick) unsalted butter

4 ounces semisweet chocolate, chopped

3 eggs, at room temperature

1 cup sugar

1/2 cup all-purpose flour

Pinch of salt

One 8-ounce package cream cheese, softened

1/2 teaspoon vanilla extract

194

*1.* Preheat the oven to 350°F. Butter and flour a 9-inch square pan.

*2.* Melt the butter and chocolate over low heat or in a microwave oven. Stir to combine and set aside to cool for 5 minutes.

*3.* Combine 2 of the eggs and 3/4 cup of the sugar in mixing bowl. Beat with an electric mixer on medium speed for 1 minute, or until well combined. Add the cooled chocolate and beat for 1 minute. Add the flour and salt and beat at low speed until just blended.

*4.* In another bowl, combine the cream cheese, remaining 1/4 cup sugar, 1 egg, and vanilla. Beat with an electric mixer on medium speed for 2 minutes, or until light and fluffy. Spread the prepared pan with the chocolate batter. Top it with the cream cheese batter and swirl the 2 layers together with a fork.

*5.* Bake for 35 minutes, or until the top is springy to the touch. Cool the brownies on a cooling rack, then cut into 12 pieces.

*Note:* The brownies can be made up to 3 days in advance and kept at room temperature, tightly covered with plastic wrap.

# White Chocolate Pecan Brownies

[ Makes 12 ]

1/2 cup (1 stick) unsalted butter, softened

1 1/3 cups (firmly packed) light brown sugar

2 eggs, at room temperature

1 teaspoon vanilla extract

1 cup all-purpose flour

Pinch of salt

1 cup chopped pecans, toasted in a 350°F. oven for 5 minutes

1 cup white chocolate pieces

1. Preheat the oven to 350°F. Butter an 8-inch square pan.
2. Combine the butter and brown sugar in a mixing bowl and beat with an electric mixer on low speed to combine. Raise the speed to high and beat for 2 minutes, or until light and fluffy. Reduce the mixer speed to medium and beat in the eggs, one at a time, and the vanilla. Reduce the speed to low and add the flour and salt. Mix until just blended. Stir in the pecans and white chocolate and spread the batter to an even layer in the prepared pan.
3. Bake for 40 minutes, or until a toothpick inserted in the center comes out clean. Cool the brownies on a cooling rack, then cut them into 12 pieces.

*Note:* The brownies can be made up to 3 days in advance and kept at room temperature, tightly covered with plastic wrap.

The combination of delicate white chocolate with the crunchy pecans make these quick and easy brownies more sophisticated than most.

*White chocolate is not officially chocolate, since it doesn't contain the thick, dark paste that remains once the cocoa butter is removed. It has the cocoa butter as its base, along with sugar and milk solids. It has a tendency to clump and should be melted over very low heat to keep it creamy.*

I've been making these lemon squares since I was a child, and they remain at the top of my list. This is also a great last-minute recipe since most of us have a lemon or two in the house, along with basic baking ingredients.

*Confectioners' sugar contains a small amount of cornstarch, which acts as a binding agent. If you make whipped cream with confectioners' sugar it will not separate as easily as cream beaten with granulated sugar.*

## Lemon Squares
[ Makes 12 ]

1/2 cup (1 stick) unsalted butter, melted

1/4 cup confectioners' sugar

1 cup plus 2 tablespoons all-purpose flour

Pinch of salt

2 eggs

1 cup granulated sugar

1/3 cup freshly squeezed lemon juice

2 teaspoons grated lemon zest

*1.* Preheat the oven to 350°F.

*2.* Combine the butter, confectioners' sugar, 1 cup of the flour, and the salt in a mixing bowl and mix thoroughly with a wooden spoon. Press the mixture into an 8-inch square pan. Bake for 20 minutes, or until set and lightly brown. Remove the crust from the oven and set aside.

*3.* Combine the eggs, granulated sugar, remaining 2 tablespoons flour, lemon juice, and lemon zest in a mixing bowl. Beat with an electric mixer on medium speed for 1 minute, or until well blended. Pour the topping over the crust and bake for 20 minutes, or until barely brown. The custard should still be soft. Cool the pan on a cooling rack, then cut into 12 pieces.

*Note:* The cookies can be refrigerated for up to 1 week, tightly covered.

# Chocolate Cranberry Biscotti

[ Makes 24 ]

4 ounces bittersweet chocolate, broken into small pieces

1 cup (firmly packed) light brown sugar

1 3/4 cups all-purpose flour

1/3 cup unsweetened cocoa

1 teaspoon baking soda

Pinch of salt

3 eggs, at room temperature

1 teaspoon vanilla extract

1 cup dried cranberries

1. Preheat the oven to 300°F. Line a baking sheet with parchment paper or wax paper.

2. Combine the chocolate and brown sugar in a food processor fitted with a steel blade and process until the chocolate is chopped very fine.

3. Sift together the flour, cocoa, baking soda, and salt and set aside. Combine the eggs and vanilla in a large mixing bowl. Beat with an electric mixer on medium speed for 1 minute. Add the chocolate mixture and beat well. Add the flour mixture and beat on low speed until a stiff dough forms. Stir in the dried cranberries. Divide the dough in half on a floured surface. Form each half into a 12-inch log. Place the logs at either side of the baking sheet, and pat them into an even shape.

4. Bake for 50 minutes, or until almost firm. Remove the pan from the oven and transfer 1 log to a cutting board. Cut the log into 3/4-inch slices with a sharp serrated knife. Arrange the slices, cut side down, on the baking sheet and bake for 35 minutes. Turn the slices over and bake for another 25 minutes, or until crisp and dry. Turn off the oven and let the biscotti cool in the oven with the oven door ajar. Remove the biscotti from the oven and store in an airtight container.

*Note:* The biscotti can be refrigerated for up to 2 weeks.

Since I moved to Nantucket I've started adding dried cranberries to many dishes; they are great in these chocolate flavored crunchy biscotti.

*Biscotti means "twice baked," and the hard cookies are part of traditional Tuscan cuisine. The name describes the unusual way in which they're made. The first baking is as a loaf, then they are sliced and baked a second time to dry them out.*

I know few people who don't adore homey, aromatic oatmeal cookies, and replacing raisins with tangy, colorful dried cranberries gives the cookies a Nantucket touch.

*An easy way to warm eggs to room temperature is to place them in a cup of hot tap water for 5 minutes, while you gather the rest of the ingredients.*

*Store soft cookies and crisp cookies in different containers to keep the crisp ones crisp.*

# Oatmeal Cranberry Cookies

[ Makes 24 ]

1 cup all-purpose flour

1 teaspoon cinnamon

1/2 teaspoon baking soda

Pinch of salt

6 tablespoons (3/4 stick) unsalted butter, softened

1/2 cup granulated sugar

1/2 cup (firmly packed) dark brown sugar

2 eggs, at room temperature

1 teaspoon vanilla extract

1 1/4 cups quick-cooking or old-fashioned oats (not instant)

1 cup dried cranberries

1 cup chopped walnuts, toasted in a 350°F. oven for 5 minutes

198

*1.* Preheat the oven to 375°F. Butter baking sheets.

*2.* Sift together the flour, cinnamon, baking soda, and salt. Place the butter, granulated sugar, and brown sugar in a large mixing bowl. Beat with an electric mixer on low speed to combine, then raise the speed to high and beat for 2 minutes, or until light and fluffy. Add the eggs and vanilla and beat for 2 minutes more. Reduce the speed to low and add the flour mixture until just blended in. Stir in the oats, cranberries, and walnuts.

*3.* Drop the batter by rounded tablespoons onto the baking sheets, spacing them 2 inches apart. Bake for 12 minutes for chewy cookies and 15 minutes for crisp cookies. Move the cookies with a spatula to a cooling rack and cool completely.

*Note:* The cookies can be stored refrigerated for up to 1 week, tightly covered.

# A Year of Island Occasions:
## Menus for a Dozen Memorable Meals

# *Celebrating the Clam*: A February Feast for Quahog Day

*W*inter days on Nantucket can be magical, when the sky is pale blue and the sun produces a clear quality of golden light. Unfortunately, those days are few, and on most winter days the island appears monochromatic. The overcast sky blends into the gray color of the weathered cedar-shake houses. It's also rare that we have significant snowfall to add sparkle and texture to the landscape, and cover the brown lawns and barren gardens. By early February, memories of December's holidays are long past, and islanders eagerly anticipate spring.

While most of the country looks to a groundhog in Pennsylvania as the prognosticator of spring's arrival, on Nantucket we have a clever clam that performs the same function—Quentin Quahog. It's the direction of a squirt, not the presence of a shadow, that determines if winter is over. When Harbormaster Dave Fronzuto opens Quentin up, if he squirts to the left we can anticipate six more weeks of winter; if he squirts to the right, winter is over.

The custom of celebrating Quahog Day on February 2nd started more than two decades ago and was the inspiration of the Harbormaster, Allen Holdgate. He continued to do the honors after retiring, and upon his death Mr. Fronzuto became Quentin's interpreter.

This menu to celebrate Quahog Day (and hopefully a squirt to the right) features clams, along with other hearty and homey winter comfort foods. In 19th-century New England, chowder parties were a favorite form of entertaining. During the summer a cauldron would be cooked over coals on the beach, and during the winter the aroma of the simmering soup would fill the house, the way this chowder does today.

*Menu:*

| | |
|---|---|
| Prosciutto and Cheese Swirls | 29 |
| Baked Clams | 37 |
| Nantucket Clam Chowder | 52 |
| Classic Caesar Salad | 46 |
| Braised Lamb Shanks | 85 |
| Buttered Egg Noodles | |
| Sautéed Spinach with Garlic | 185 |
| Flourless Chocolate Nut Torte | 185 |

# Signs of Spring: A Daffodil Day Tailgate Picnic

$\mathcal{R}$egardless of the official date of the equinox, Nantucketers maintain that spring arrives the last Saturday in April on Daffodil Day. By early morning the cobblestoned streets of town are filled with more than a hundred daffodil-decked vintage cars and their owners, most of whom dress to harmonize with the style and age of their vehicles. Throngs of people wander between the lines of cars, chatting with the owners and photographing the sea of yellow blooms.

At noon the slow-moving parade, which became part of the Daffodil Day festivities in 1978, starts the seven-mile trip on Milestone Road to Main Street in 'Sconset. Along the way the cars' occupants wave and beep their horns at the hundreds of onlookers.

When the parade ends the party begins. The small village of 'Sconset becomes the island's block party for the afternoon.

Most of the car-owners from the parade spread blankets and set up tables, and farther down on Main Street spectators do the same. There are picnics with themes vying for prizes awarded by the Nantucket Island Chamber of Commerce, the official sponsor of the festival since 1980, and then there are totally lavish picnics celebrating the festive spirit of the event.

The festival began in 1975, a year after the late Jean MacAusland, a summer resident and wife of *Gourmet* magazine founder Earle MacAusland, persuaded the Nantucket Garden Club to invite the American Daffodil Society to show on the island. Each year the club planted drifts of bulbs along Milestone Road, and in the early 1980s Mrs. MacAusland donated eight tons of bulbs from the Netherlands to speed the island's coverage of blooms on other major roads.

It's estimated that members of the Nantucket Garden Club are responsible for planting three million daffodils on the roads of Nantucket, and that number is probably matched by the bulbs in private gardens.

This picnic menu celebrates some of the foods that are harbingers of spring, and it can be easily transported.

---

*Menu:*

| | |
|---|---|
| Cream of Asparagus Soup | *55* |
| Herbed Sausage and Tomato Quiche | *124* |
| Moroccan Chicken Salad | *68* |
| Jambalaya Salad | *66* |
| Lemon Squares | *196* |
| Rhubarb Crumb Pie | *187* |

*True* sports fishermen, like my friends Jenny and Chad Whitlock, maintain that pound-for-pound there is no fiercer a fighting fish than bluefish. The middle of May is when schools of bluefish arrive off the beaches of Nantucket, after swimming north for the summer from the waters off the North Carolina coast. True aficionados have their secret spots on the island's south shore, where they don waders to start reeling in the fish at dawn or dusk.

Bluefish can be caught all summer off the island's beaches, but the greatest concentrations are in May and then again around Columbus Day, when the schools are returning to warmer southern waters. It's in the fall that the Angler's Club stages its yearly bluefish tournament.

Bluefish are caught with artificial lures, and while the fish can weigh up to 20 pounds, the most flavorful fillets are from those weighing five to seven pounds. Bluefish run with striped bass, another spring delicacy. Fishermen can tell if it's a bass on their lines after a few seconds. The bass put up little resistance to being reeled in.

But bluefish fight to the end. They jump out of the water and shake their heads. Fishermen warn that even once on land the bluefish are still fighting and that they should be handled carefully by their tails to avoid contact with their sharp teeth.

In the same way that friends of gardeners rarely have to buy zucchini or tomatoes in August, since they benefit from too many vegetables ripening at the same moment, so friends of fishermen are gifted in late May with beautiful bluefish fillets.

Many people shy away from bluefish, thinking of the fish as strongly flavored. But I've created many converts by serving freshly caught, delicately flavored grilled bluefish as the centerpiece of a late May dinner. Since there's such an abundance of fish at that time I smoke part of the cache, some of it for small bluefish cakes now, some for bluefish pâtés later in the summer.

Late May is when the island's strawberry crop is usually ripe for the picking, so this menu ends with a simple dessert that showcases the sweetness of the local berries.

*Menu:*

| | |
|---|---|
| Smoked Bluefish Cakes | 22 |
| Crudité Basket with Tuscan White Bean Spread | 166 |
| Greek Lemon Egg Soup | 57 |
| Grilled Bluefish | 102 |
| Sun-Dried Tomato Spread | 167 |
| Summer Vegetable Custard | 136 |
| Hash-Brown Potato Salad with Bacon and Onion | 154 |
| Fresh Berries with Lemon Mousse | 193 |

*P*art of the joy of exploring Nantucket's miles of pristine sandy beaches is that many secluded picnic spots are accessible by plodding along the sand slowly in a car with four-wheel drive on partially deflated tires. Buying the necessary Oversand Driving Permit is a yearly ritual. Many islanders stack the brightly colored stickers side by side on the bumper to show the age of the car the way that rings show the age of a tree.

One of the most popular drives starts at Wauwinet and meanders up the crescent coast toward the lighthouse at Great Point. Located at the northeastern tip of the island, the current lighthouse is a replica of the one built in 1818 that was destroyed by a storm in 1984. Along the way are many spots to spread a blanket or set up a picnic table, and the bonus of using the car is that the picnic can be more elaborate than a hand-carried one.

The 1100 acres of wildlife refuge that includes the barrier beaches of Coatue are the property of the Trustees of Reservations. The group is the country's oldest land trust, and the organization conducts its own tours of the area during the summer months.

While Great Point is an idyllic site to spend a leisurely afternoon, another popular option is to drive for a sunset picnic at Smith Point at the western end of the island at Madaket.

This picnic menu is Asian in inspiration, and many of the dishes are ones I developed a few years ago for *Coastal Living* magazine. The use of Asian ingredients is consistent with the island's culinary history. The whaling ships visited Asia and the South Pacific, and there are many references to curries and ginger being served at mid-19th century dinner parties.

These dishes can be mixed and matched in any way, if you want a less abundant number of choices.

*Menu:*

| | |
|---|---|
| Grilled Chinese Chicken Wings | 28 |
| Ginger Gravlax with Cilantro Mustard Sauce | 21 |
| Asian Steak Salad | 74 |
| Thai Lobster Salad | 91 |
| Stir-Fried Vegetable Salad | 140 |
| Thai Cucumber Salad | 134 |
| Jasmine Rice Salad | 156 |
| Ginger Cake | 180 |

# *Summer Soiree* : The Twilight Cocktail Party

*M*odes of entertaining on Nantucket change with the seasons. During the more leisurely fall and winter months islanders usually entertain at brunches and small dinner parties. But for July and August the number of invited guests expands with the island's population, which grows from its year-round base of ten thousand to upwards of fifty thousand.

During this hectic short summer season the most popular form of entertaining is at a large cocktail party, and many people who entertain at no other time of the year are likely to host one. For summer residents who might occupy their houses for only a few weeks or weekends, a cocktail party allows them to gather a large group of friends to renew contact after a winter of living dispersed around the country.

Cocktail parties are flexible, and can grow to include the numerous house guests who might be staying with invited friends. They also allow guests to accept several invitations for the same evening or stop by for a short visit en route to a restaurant for dinner.

When I plan cocktail party hors d'oeuvres, my principle is that the food should be abundant enough that guests can leave feeling as full as after dinner if they so desire. The only distinction between the menu for a cocktail party and a buffet is that no utensils are needed to eat the food. Another menu-planning goal is variety; this menu includes vegetarian, seafood, and meat dishes. Most of these hors d'oeuvres can be passed, while other dishes can be placed around on tables for the duration of the party.

*Menu:*

Crudité Basket:
  Dill and Scallion Dip                            *164*

  Blue Cheese Dip                            *165*

Southwest Miniature Lobster Cakes         *18*

Baked Shrimp Toast Rolls                 *23*

Pesto Quesadillas                         *24*

Chicken Satay with Spicy Thai Peanut Sauce    *27*

Herbed Chèvre and Roasted Pepper Spirals     *25*

Caramelized Onion Mini-Quiche            *125*

Southwest Smoked Salmon Pinwheels       *20*

# *Star-Spangled Supper*: A Grilled Dinner Prior to the Fourth of July Fireworks

*W*hile there were no battles fought here, more than fifteen hundred Nantucketers lost their lives during the Revolutionary War. Celebrating the country's independence has been part of the island's tradition since the birth of the nation.

In addition to the participation by its citizens, Nantucket's other tie to the fight for independence is that the three ships that were raided in the Boston Tea Party in 1773 sailed from the island laden with whale oil on their previous voyage.

For New Englanders, Independence Day has always been treated as a major holiday, filled with activities from morning to night. July 4th on Nantucket remains a day of old-fashioned fun that appeals to islanders and visitors alike.

In the morning Main Street is the site of myriad activities. There is a pie-eating contest, the town's fire trucks square off for a water contest, and children line up to have their faces painted by local artists. Decorated bicycles parade down the cobblestones, and local musicians serenade.

The afternoon is a time for personal celebrations and trips to the beach, before trekking to Jetties Beach for the spectacular evening fireworks that light the sky and reflect off the water. Sponsored by the island's Visitor's Services department, the beach event includes a band concert for sing-along fun.

Grill-outs are a historically part of Nantucket's Fourth of July. The earliest settlers termed their outdoor barbecues *Squantum*, and credited the tradition to the last Native American woman to live on the shores of Boston harbor.

This menu for a late afternoon meal, before the trip to Jetties Beach, includes foods in our patriotic hues of red, white, and blue.

---

*Menu:*

| | |
|---|---|
| Cranberry Maple Spareribs | 78 |
| Pesto Quesadillas | 24 |
| Red Pepper Bisque | 56 |
| Grilled Steaks with Southwest Corn Sauce | 76 |
| Janet's Fourth of July Potato Salad | 153 |
| Celery Seed Slaw | 131 |
| Sautéed Cherry Tomatoes | 144 |
| Blueberry Crème Fraîche Tart | 188 |

Many island traditions began at the instigation of a resident. Just as Daffodil Day can be credited to Jean MacAusland, the Opera House Cup Race in August will always remain linked to Gwen and Harold Gaillard.

The Gaillards moved to Nantucket shortly after World War II and opened the island's first fine dining restaurant, The Opera House. For nearly thirty years Harold monitored the door while Gwen supervised the kitchen, and fishing captains dined next to Palm Beach celebrities. The late Chick Walsh, who became proprietor of highly acclaimed 21 Federal, was the bartender. He recalled how the Gaillards brought a sense of cosmopolitan style and flair to the restaurant and the food they served.

The Opera House was a center for the island's social life, as well as its most popular late-night watering hole. It was where residents learned what notables were vacationing on the island, and all the concomitant gossip.

When Harold Gaillard passed away in 1973 the loyal local clientele wanted to memorialize him. At the time, there was no yearly competition for the large number of single-hulled wooden boats that sailed out of the harbor on charter or for pleasure. Gwen volunteered a trophy, and The Opera House Cup Race was launched. The first year there were about fifteen local boats; there are now more than seventy-five boats entered, ranging in size from a 26-foot sloop to the 126-foot *Endeavor*.

In 1980 the Opera House Cup Race became one leg of the National Schooner Race Association and in 1990 one of the premier events of the Wooden Boat Regatta Series. The race also generates income for Nantucket Community Sailing, which provides affordable lessons to both children and adults.

Watching the race from boats moored in the harbor provides a front-row seat, as well as a great venue for an elegant picnic on the deck. This menu includes both tomatoes and corn, two crops at their height in August that should not be missed.

---

*Menu:*

| | |
|---|---|
| Crudité Basket with Two Salmon Spread | 163 |
| Tomato and Mozzarella Salad with Oregano | 45 |
| Smoked Turkey Salad | 71 |
| Lobster and Corn Salad | 90 |
| Gazpacho Salad | 130 |
| Sweet Potato Salad with Mustard Dressing | 155 |
| Peanut Butter Mousse Pie | 192 |

*L*abor Day no longer signals that Nantucket will begin settling into a slower pace for fall. September and October have become even more popular than June for weddings, and an increasing number of these weddings have no familial ties to the island.

Some couples decide to marry on Nantucket because of the significance trips to the island had on their emerging romance. Other couples think of the island as a romantic site that their guests would enjoy visiting for a destination wedding.

Many families rent a large home or complex of homes as headquarters for the wedding week. The wedding party stays in the bedrooms and a tent can be erected on the lawn for the ceremony and/or reception. The tent frequently serves a second function on Sunday morning as the site of a farewell brunch.

By changing from white linens to a pattern that ties to the colors of the flowers chosen for the wedding, the look of the interior of the tent can be changed to a more casual one appropriate for a brunch.

The time and nature of the brunch is influenced by the wedding it follows. If the wedding reception was an evening multi-course seated dinner, then chances are the brunch is merely a continental breakfast with large platters of fruit and freshly baked pastries. If, however, the reception was earlier in the day or a cocktail buffet, I assume that guests will arrive anticipating a heartier meal such as the menu listed below.

*Menu:*

The commercial scalloping season, which began on Nantucket in 1881, spans the months of November to March. But island residents begin to enjoy the island's renowned tiny morsels when Family Scalloping begins on the first day of October.

Some gatherers don't use boats of any kind. They protect themselves with waders and go into shallow, sheltered areas to rake scallops out from the eel grass. Other local aficionados will leave their moorings before dawn. Like commercial scallopers, they throw dredges over the side of their A-frame boats, and haul them in by hand.

218

They place their catch on a culling board in the center of the boat and pick through the eel grass to pluck out scallops of the right size. To be legal, scallops have to show a growth ring on the shell; smaller ones are thrown back into the water as seed for next year's crop.

After work the scallop fishermen return home to pry apart the decorative shells and scrape out the prized mollusk. The marshmallow-shaped nugget that we savor is actually the scallop's adductor muscle that allows it to scurry around on the ocean floor.

Our bay scallops, *Argopecten irradians*, are a relative latecomer in shellfish popularity and ranked far below oysters and lobster during the height of the whaling era. There are references to scallops before the Civil War, but it was not common to find recipes in New England cookbooks until the 1870s.

The fame of scallops grew as they were marketed to larger cities. A writer in the New York *Herald* in the late 19th century touted the flavor as "indefinable lusciousness not possessed by any fish or fruit."

Scallops are fast and easy to cook as well as being versatile. They are delicious both hot and cold. The only caveat is to sauté or grill them quickly with high heat. They toughen if overcooked.

*Menu:*

| | |
|---|---|
| Nantucket Scallop Ceviche in Cherry Tomatoes | *19* |
| Smoked Trout Spread on Cucumber Slices | *162* |
| Fennel Salad | *47* |
| Sautéed Scallops with Leeks | *100* |
| Fall Tomato Gratin | *143* |
| Warm Chocolate Tortes | *184* |

*C*oncern for preserving Nantucket's natural beauty and open spaces dates back more than thirty years, and one of the island's jewels is Sanford Farm and its adjoining tracts of land, Ram Pasture and The Woods. On crisp fall days, islanders frequently meet and hike at least some of the more than six miles of trails, and the hiking works up an appetite for a hearty lunch.

The credit for amassing the more than seven hundred acres of wetlands, grasslands, and forests is shared by the public and private sectors. Ram Pasture and The Woods were purchased in 1971 by the membership-supported Nantucket Conservation Foundation. In 1985, the Foundation joined forces with the Nantucket Islands Land Bank Commission, a county governmental agency, to secure Sanford Farm from the estate of Mrs. Anne Sanford.

Archeological excavations have found many Native American artifacts on the property that lead us to believe this was an important settlement from the island's inhabited beginnings, due to its proximity to both the salt water of the ocean and the fresh water of Hummock Pond. The land was part of the common land shared by the original band of twenty-seven English settlers for grazing their sheep.

Two of the most popular trails are "the loop," which can be walked in less than an hour, and the more ambitious three-mile hike to the barn in Ram Pasture, from which there is a panoramic ocean view that stretches from Cisco Beach to Madaket on a clear day.

Along the way are examples of many indigenous flowers, trees, and shrubs. During the fall, hikers pass heads of Queen Anne's lace and Joe Pye Weed already drying in the cool air, as well as brilliant red hips on *Rosa rugosa*.

While luscious summer tomatoes are a memory by early October, this luncheon of hearty, homey dishes includes the produce still available locally in the fall, such as beets and potatoes.

---

*Menu:*

| | |
|---|---|
| Muffuletta Quesadillas | 30 |
| White Bean Soup with Rosemary and Spinach | 67 |
| Red Cabbage Slaw | 132 |
| Shepherd's Pie | 86 |
| Maple-Glazed Beets | 149 |
| Jodi Levesque's Carrot Cake | 182 |

# *Party with the Pilgrims*: An Updated Thanksgiving Dinner

*It's* likely that Thanksgiving has been celebrated on Nantucket since Thomas Macy and the first colonists joined the island's Native American population 1659. It was in 1621 that Governor William Bradford declared a day of Thanksgiving in Plymouth and began the tradition all New England villages adopted to celebrate the conclusion of what they hoped would be an abundant harvest season.

At first, Thanksgiving was celebrated at any time from mid-October to the end of November and almost exclusively in New England. Connecticut native Harriet Beecher Stowe promoted Thanksgiving as a national holiday in *Oldtown Folks,* after her abolitionist activities were no longer necessary. However the holiday was not set as the last Thursday in November until Franklin Delano Roosevelt's presidency.

During the 19th century, Thanksgiving outranked Christmas as the premier annual holiday for most New Englanders. Turkey, native to America and a luxury in England, was chosen during the early colonial days as the centerpiece of the feast, although it was common to also serve pork or beef. Pies became the traditional dessert since they were imbedded in New Englanders' British background.

Thanksgiving on Nantucket energizes the island after more than a month of the slower pace that anticipates winter. Many summer residents return for the long holiday weekend, and visitors gather their families in rented homes.

While almost all of the island's restaurants are open for weekend dinners, there are few options for those who might want to dine out on Thanksgiving Day, so there is a last-minute rush of activity at the supermarkets as people arrive on Wednesday night.

Even though my Thanksgiving menu still features a turkey, over the years I've created some new twists for traditional side dishes, at least some of which are among most people's family favorites. The butternut squash puree, for example, is flavored with Chinese five-spice powder and hoisin sauce in lieu of the traditional brown sugar, and the yams are flavored with citrus fruits.

*Menu:*

| | |
|---|---|
| Cheddar Crackers | 26 |
| Cream of Acorn Squash Soup | 60 |
| Turkey (made your favorite way) | |
| Corn Pudding | 147 |
| Braised Red Cabbage | 148 |
| Asian Butternut Squash Puree | 150 |
| Green Beans with Mushroom Sauce | 142 |
| Yams à la Churchill | 159 |
| Cranberry Chutney | 177 |
| Cranberry Apple Pie | 190 |
| Chocolate Caramel Pecan Pie | 191 |

# *Fireside Feast* : A Christmas Stroll Brunch

*During* the Christmas holidays the streets of Nantucket look as if they are plucked from the pages of a novel by Dickens. The facades of houses, especially those in the historic district, are decorated with elaborate swags of evergreens and decorated wreaths on the doors. Sprigs of holly, bayberry, and colorful red native berries replace summer annuals in window boxes and planters.

The Friday of Thanksgiving weekend is the official start of the island's holiday festivities. Right after sunset is the lighting of the Main Street Christmas trees, decorated with large, old-fashioned colored lights. However, the concentration of holiday partying is reserved for Christmas Stroll, the first weekend in December.

The Nantucket Island Chamber of Commerce launched Christmas Stroll in 1974 as a way to lure shoppers to the island. It's now a beloved island tradition, and the panoply of activities involve the community.

Santa arrives on a Coast Guard boat and is then announced by a Town Crier as he is driven up Main Street in a horse-drawn carriage. Victorian-costumed carolers add lilting music to the air, and businesses vie for prizes for the best tree and window decorations. Other trees are decorated by grade school classes and community groups.

Christmas Stroll is also the last weekend that many of the island's summer residents use their houses before closing them for the winter. That makes it a time to entertain one more time, to invite house guests, and to say farewell to the island and many of their friends until spring.

This brunch menu can be served as either a buffet or a seated meal, and the foods incorporate some island specialties such as lobster and cranberries.

---

## Menu:

| | |
|---|---|
| Everett Reid's Smoked Lobster Pancake | 40 |
| Lobster Bisque | 54 |
| Grilled Chicken Hash | 112 |
| Ginger-Glazed Carrots | 145 |
| Sautéed Zucchini Pancakes | 146 |
| Christmas Stroll Fruit Compote | 126 |
| Cranberry Cake | 183 |

# About the Author

For the past 25 years, Ellen Brown has spent her life as the consummate "foodie." She is now chef/owner of Nantucket Cuisine, a catering firm launched in 2000.

She gained national limelight in 1982 as the founding food editor of *USA Today*, and she was previously senior feature writer for the Cincinnati Enquirer, where her areas of coverage included restaurants, food, art, interior design, and fashion.

She is the author of *All Wrapped Up*, published in 1998 by Broadway Books, as well as the IACP Award-winning *Gourmet Gazelle Cookbook* (Bantam Books, 1989), which was on the *Cook's* magazine best-seller list for four months.

Her book credits also include *Cooking with the New American Chefs* (Harper & Row, 1985), *The Great Chefs of Chicago* (Avon Books, 1985), *Southwest Tastes* (HP Books, 1987), and *Great Chefs of the East* (Great Chefs Publishing, 1995). In addition, she served as editor for *Great Chefs Cook American* and *Great Chefs Cook Italian* (Ellen Rolfes Books, 1995) and *The Junior League Centennial Cookbook* (Doubleday, 1996).

Her writing has appeared in more than two dozen publications, including *The Washington Post*, *The Los Angeles Times* syndicate, the Prodigy computer network, *Coastal Living*, *Bon Appetit*, *Art Culinaire*, *Museum and Arts Washington*, *Texas Monthly*, *The Baltimore Sun*, *The San Francisco Chronicle*, *Ft. Lauderdale News Sentinel*, *Tables*, *Good Food*, *Dossier*, *Showcase* and *Diversion*.

In 1985, she was honored by *Cook's* magazine, who selected her for inclusion in the prestigious "Who's Who of Cooking in America," and profiles of her have appeared in *The Washington Post*, *The Detroit News*, *Coastal Living*, and *The Miami Herald*.

She was the vice-chair of the National Capital Area chapter of the American Institute of Wine and Food, and is a former board member of Les Dames d'Escoffier and the New England Culinary Institute. She began splitting her time between Nantucket and Washington, DC, in 1991, and became a year-round islander in 1997.

*Notes*

*Notes*

*Notes*